ANIMAL ADVENTURES

Coloring book

Thank you so much for purchasing my coloring book. Your support means the world to me!
I hope it brings you joy and inspiration as much as it did for me while creating it.

Warm regards,

Shekira

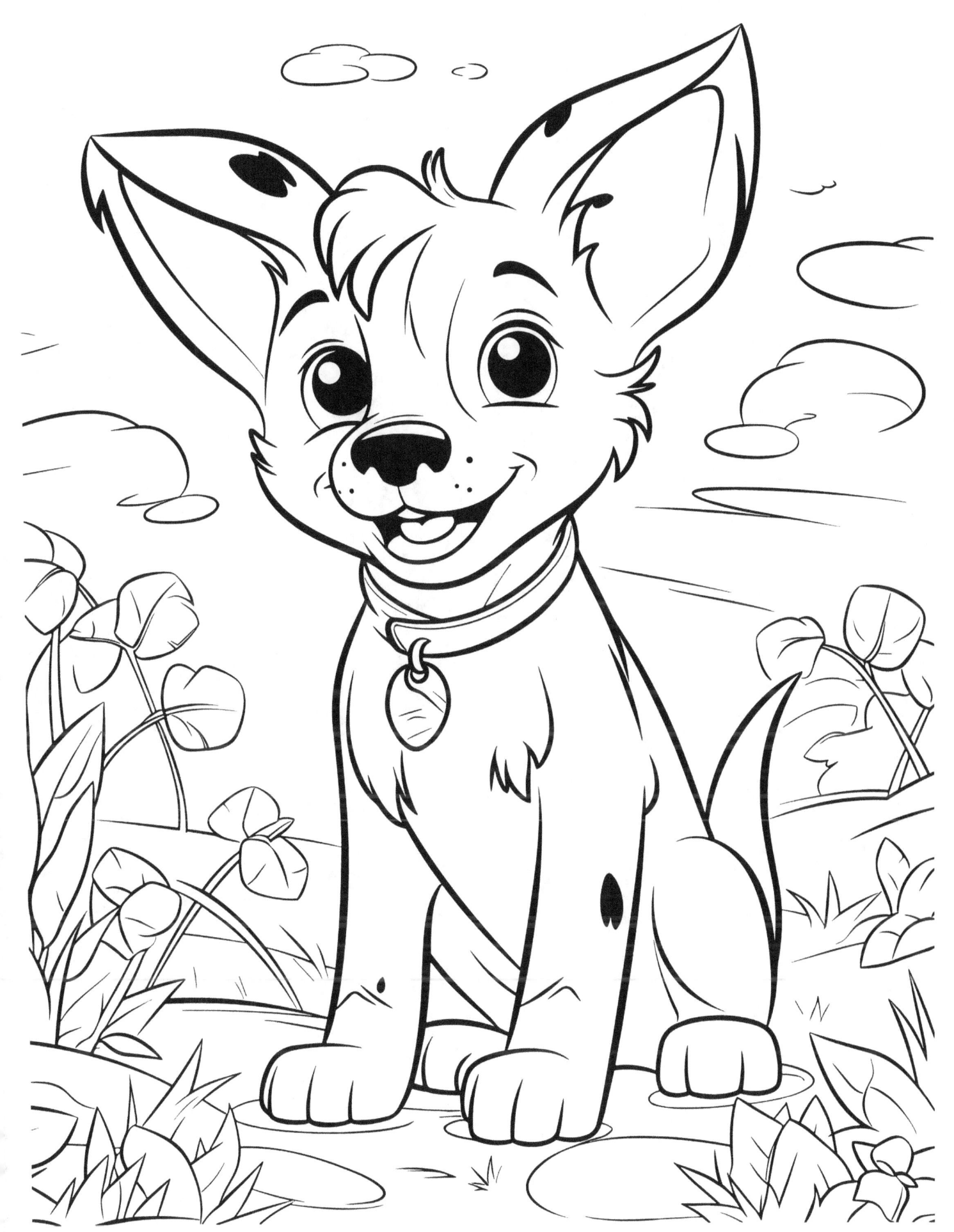

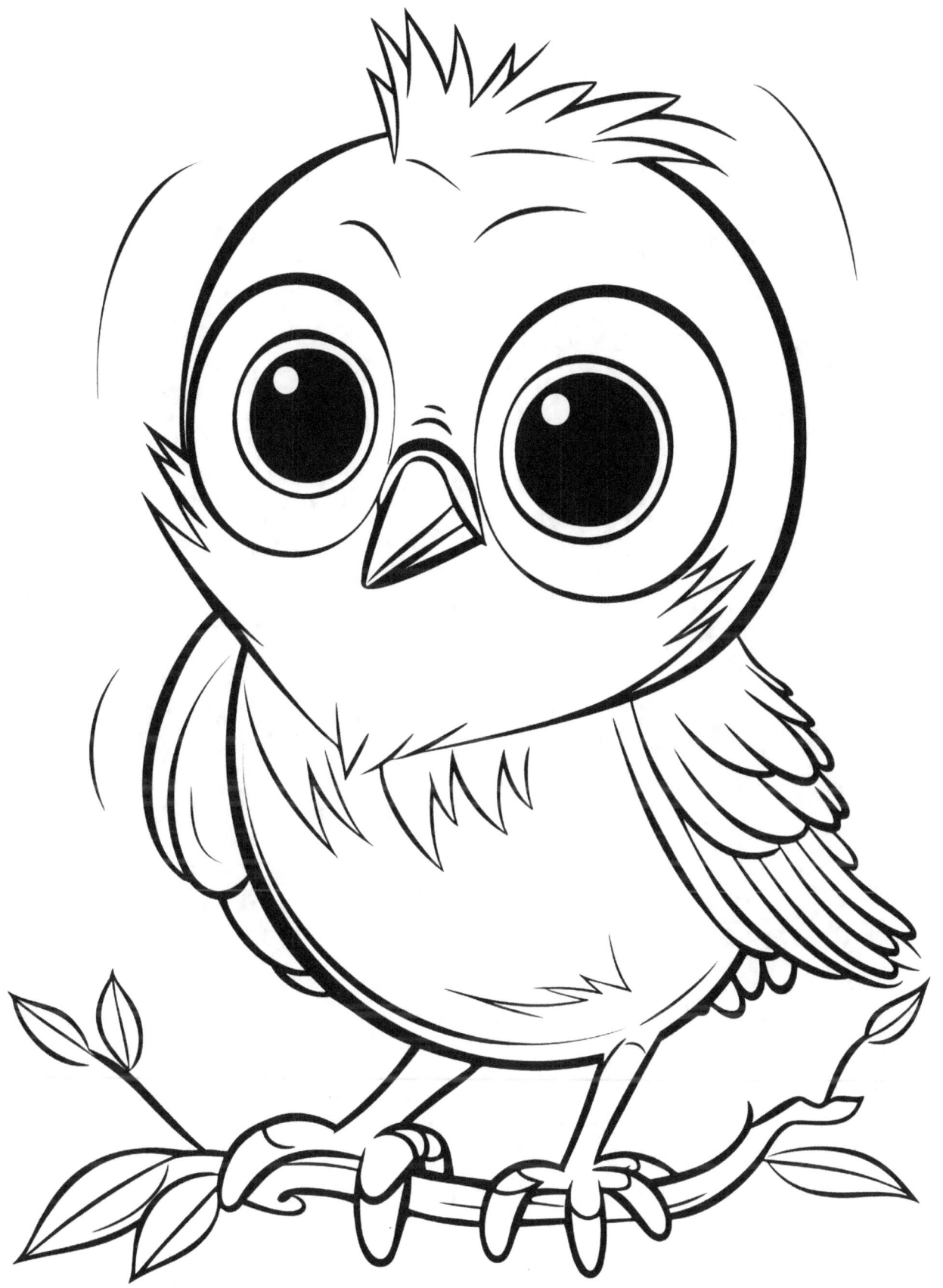

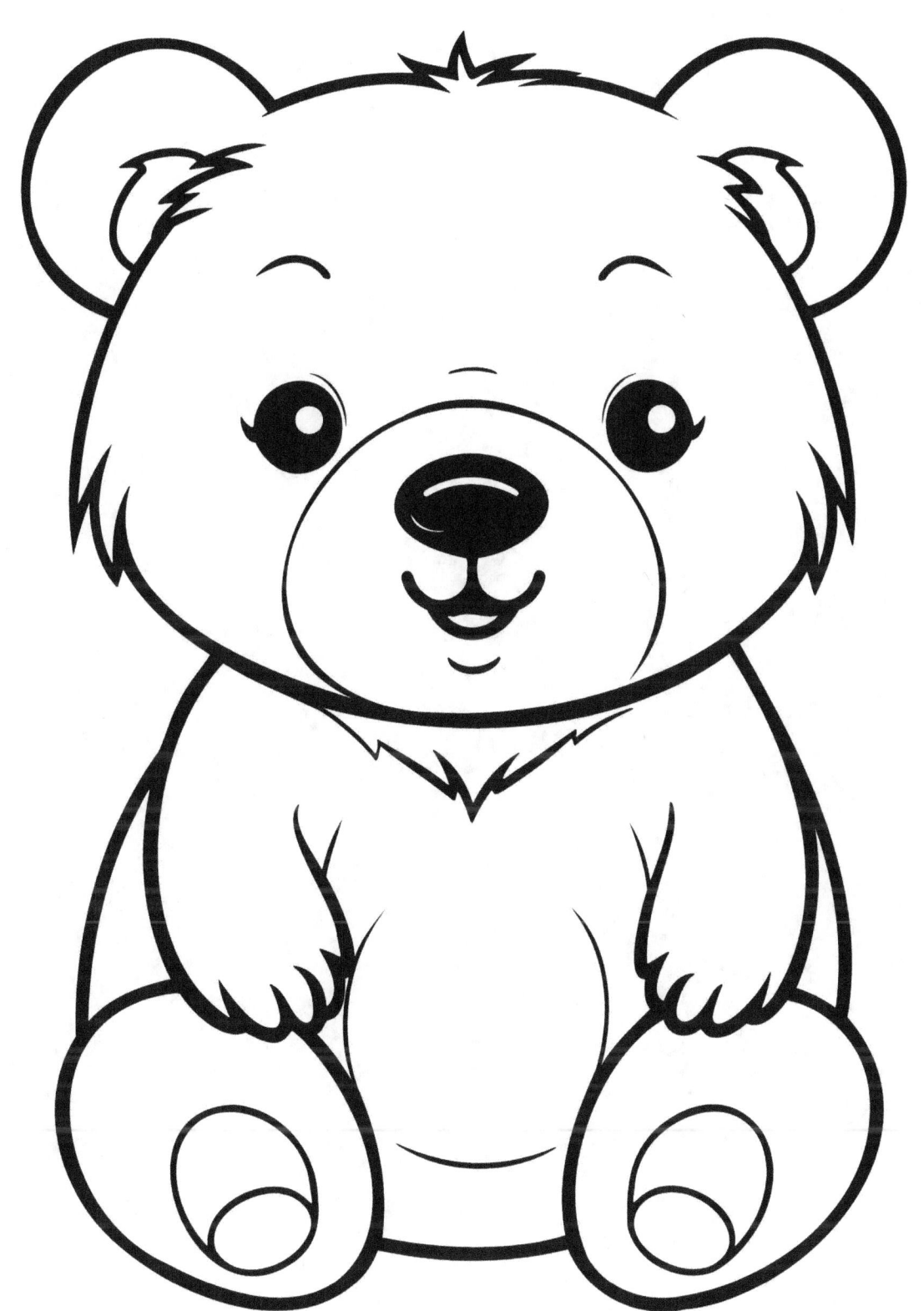

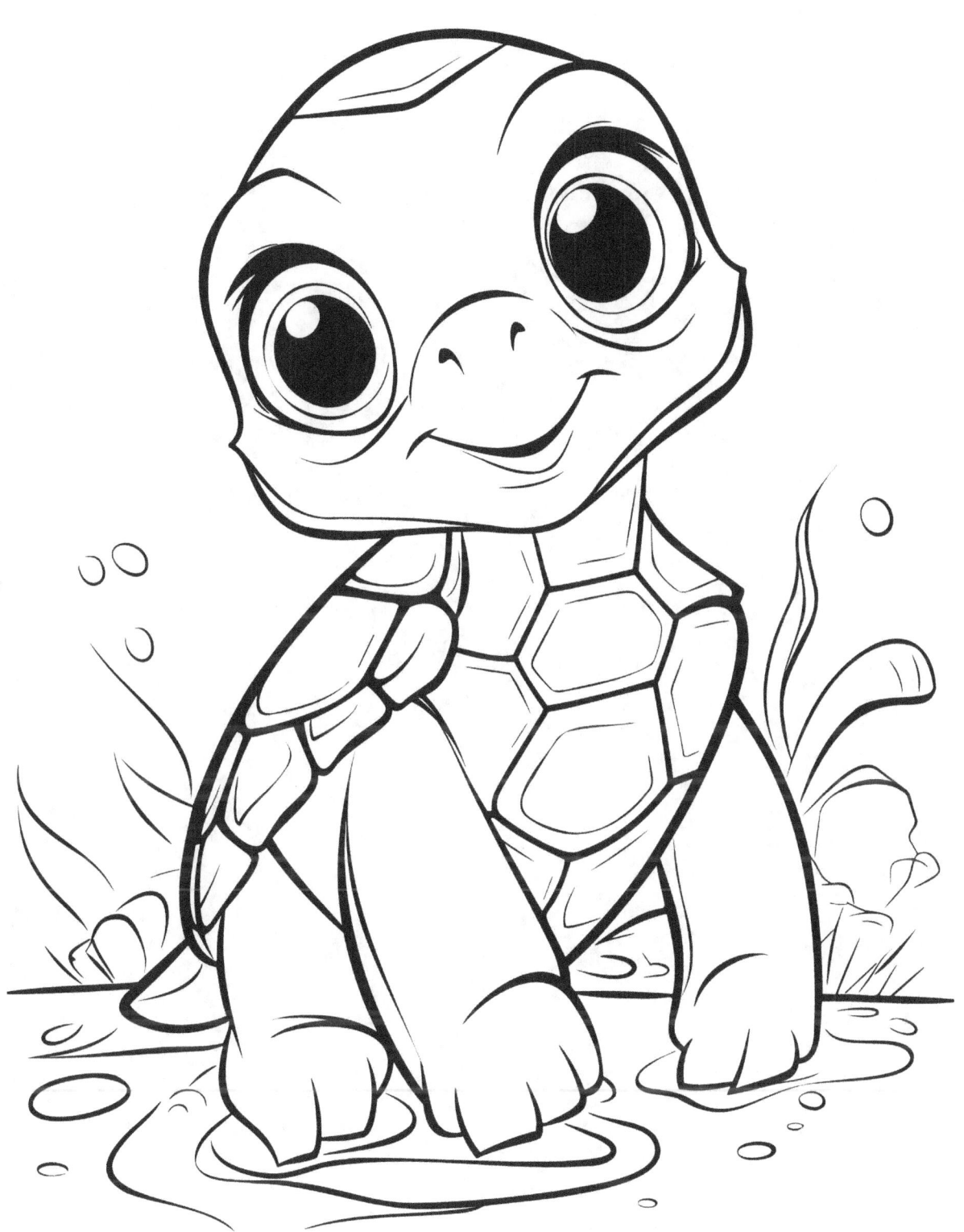

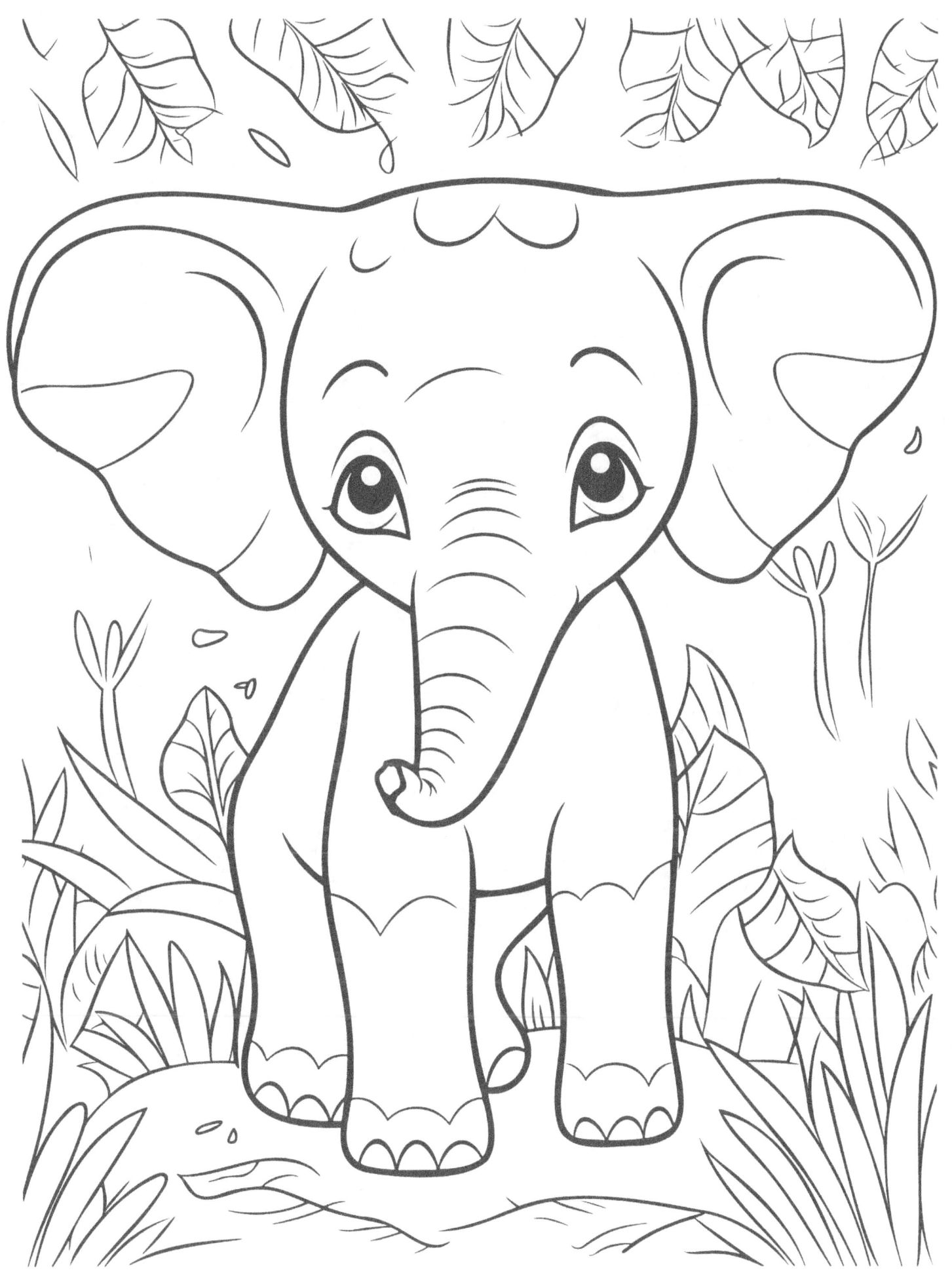

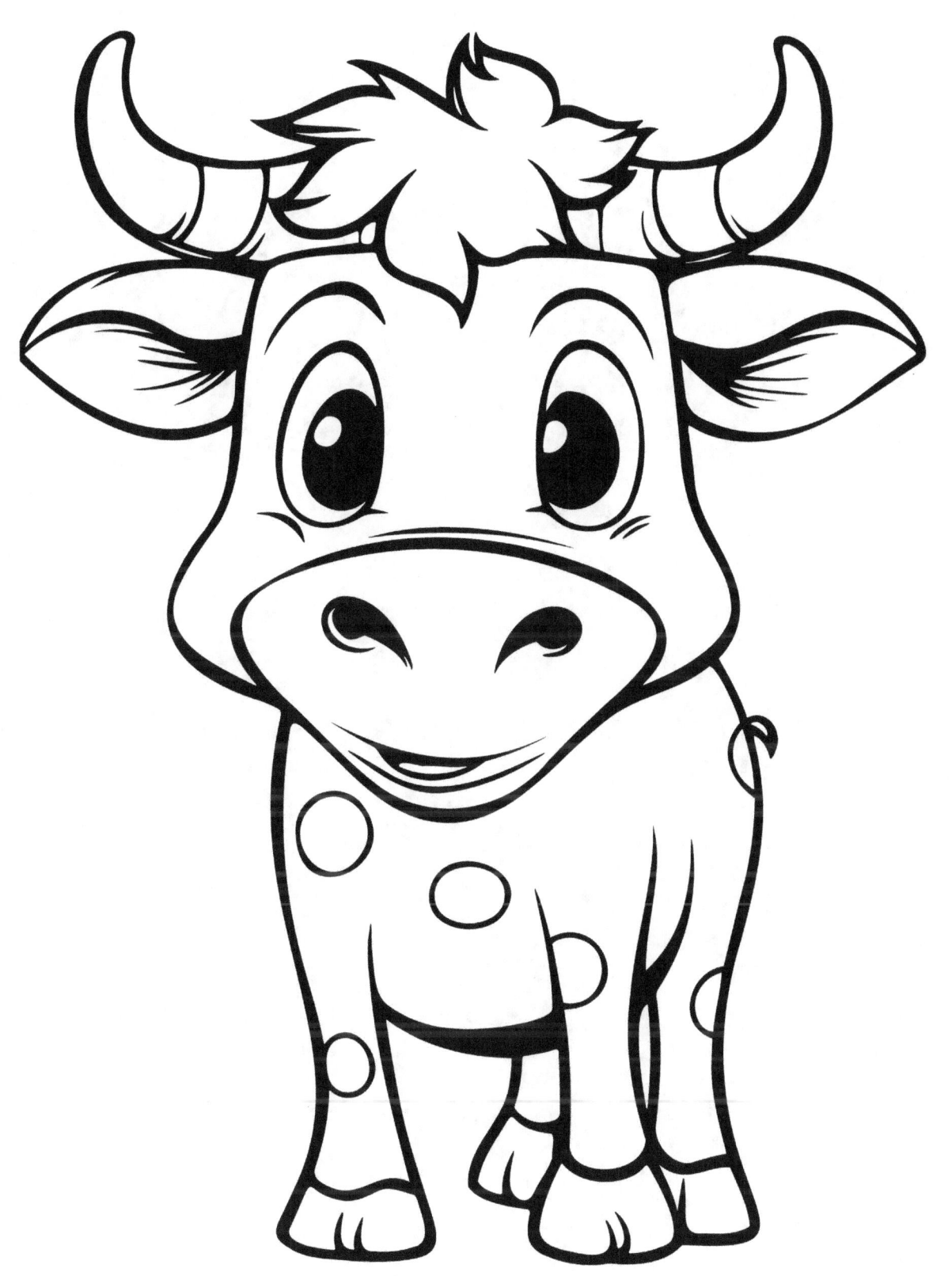

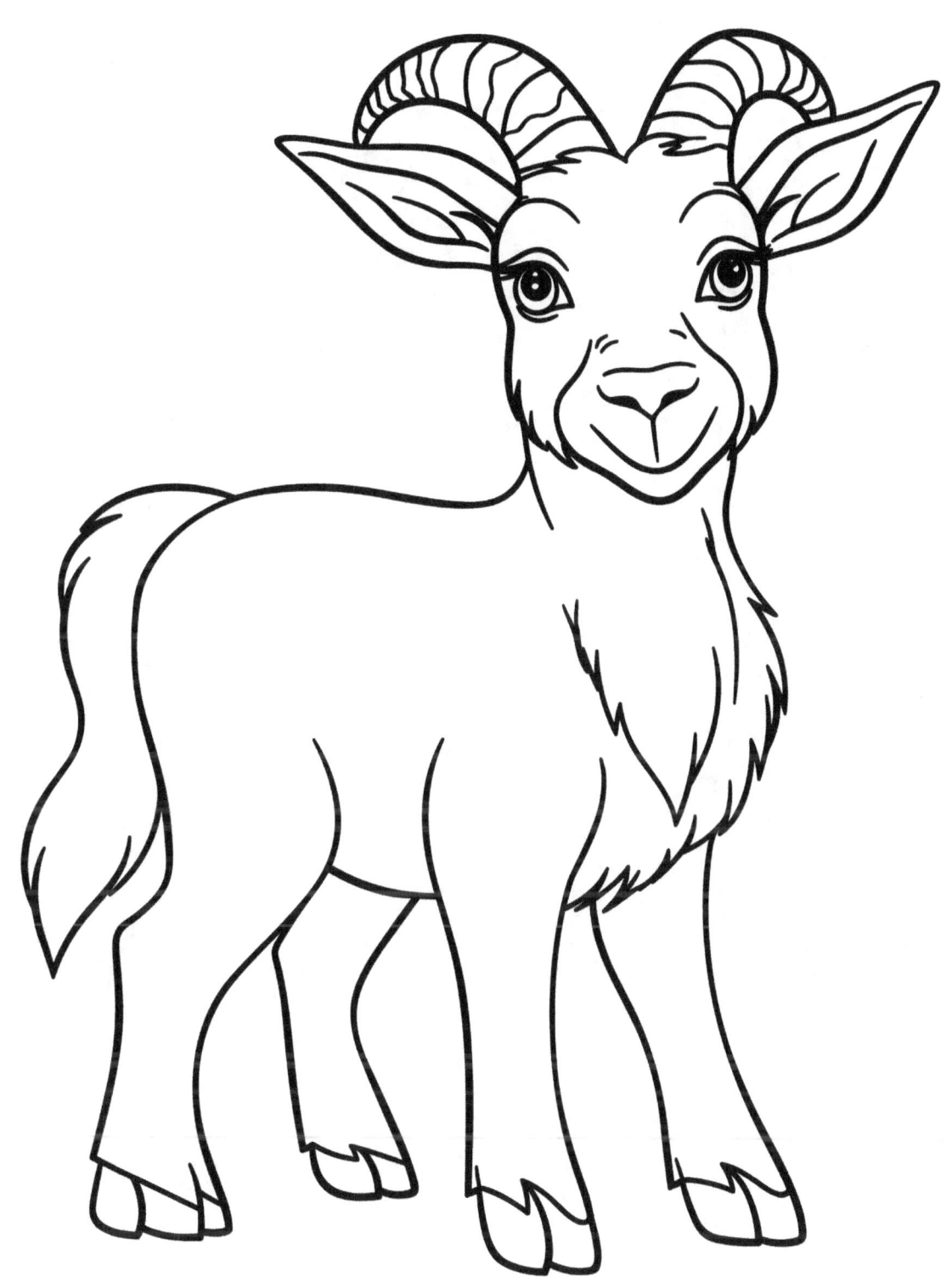

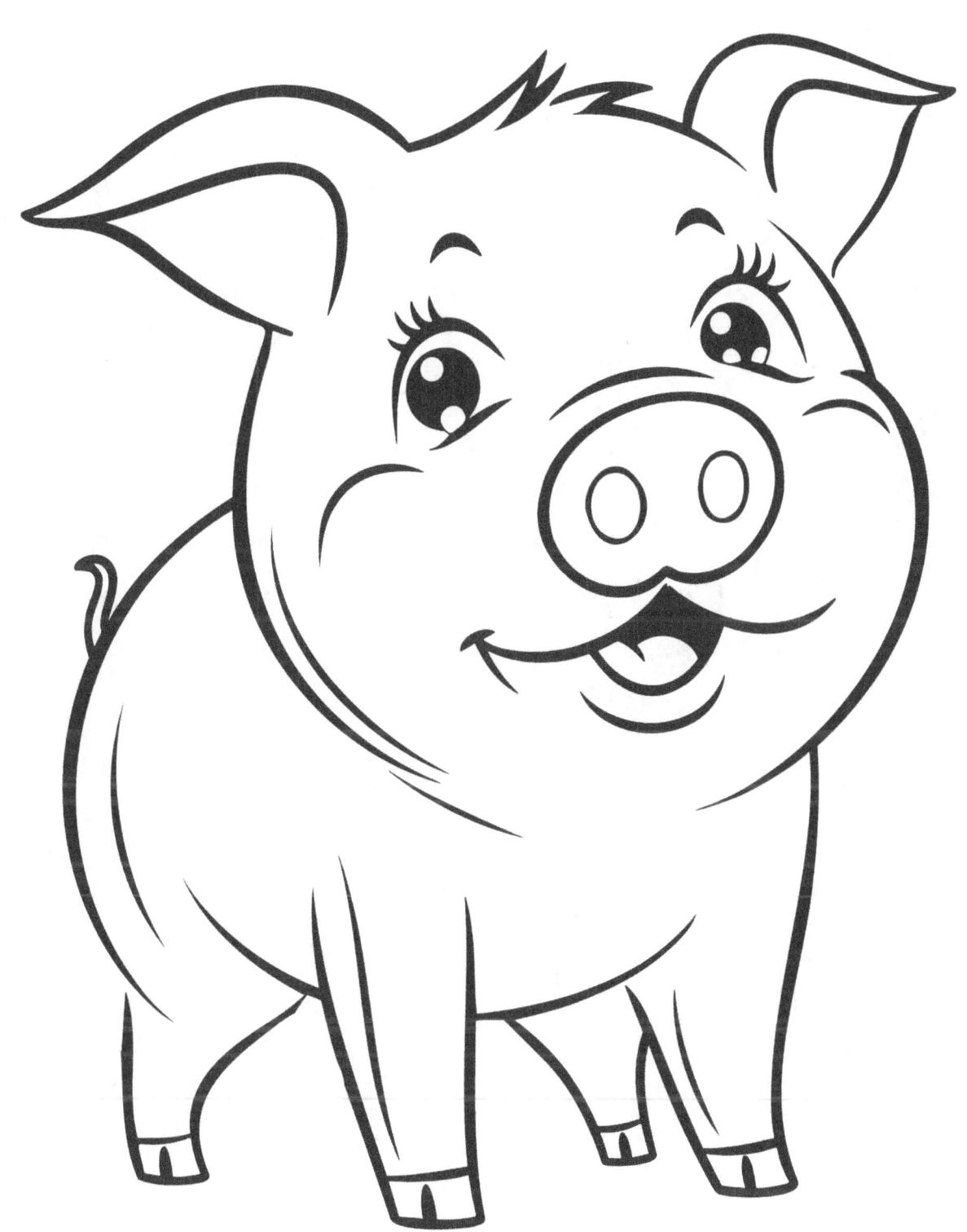

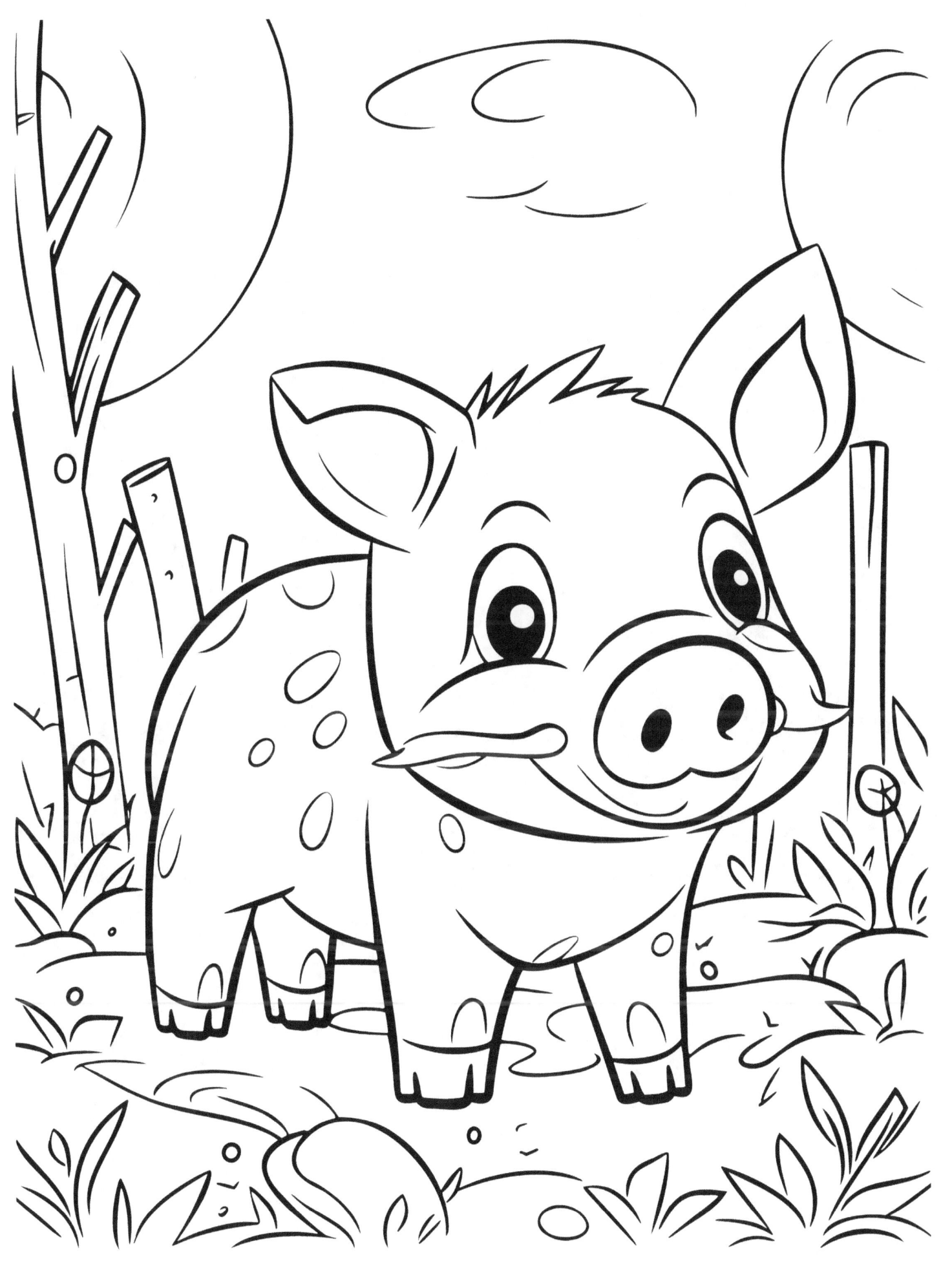

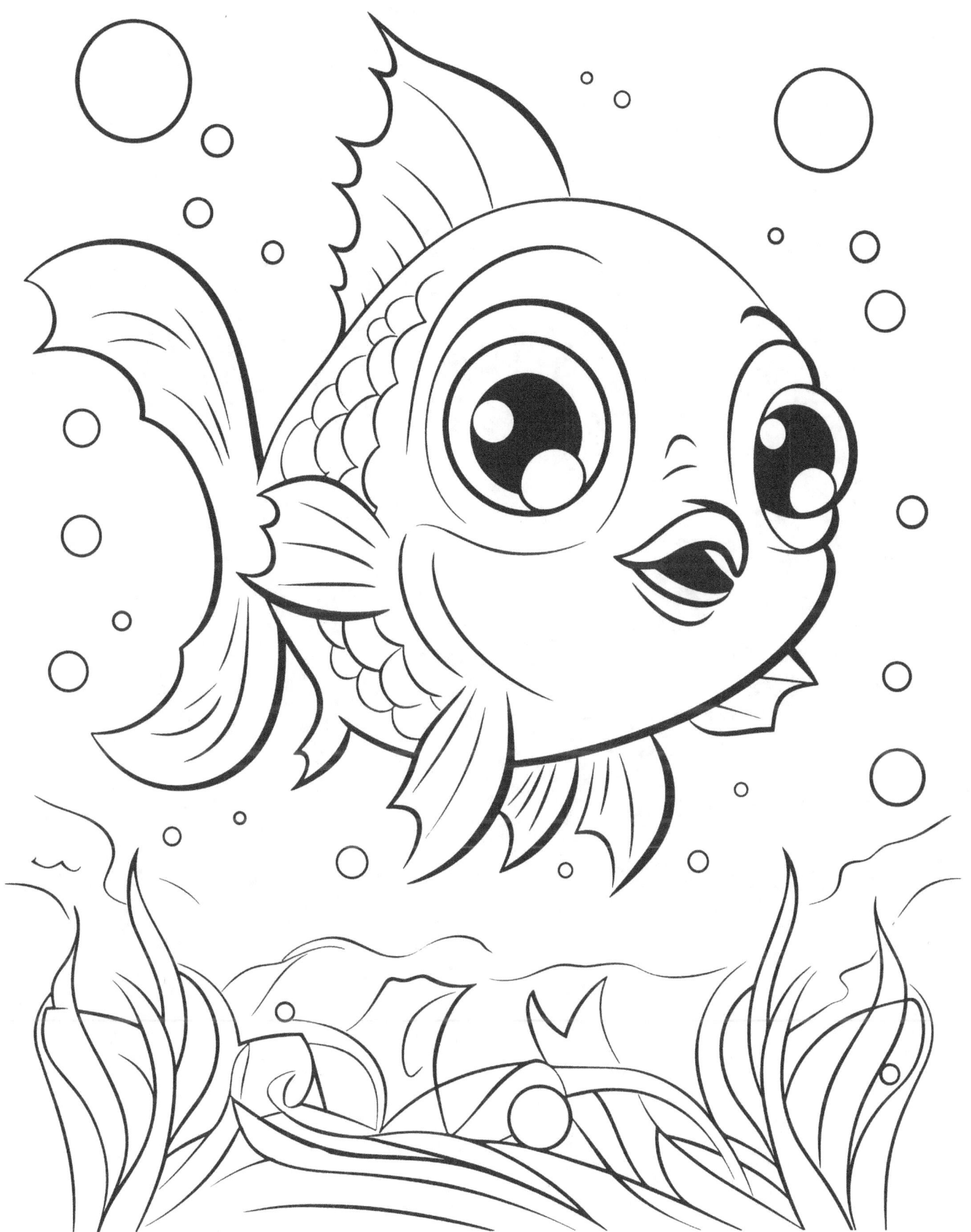

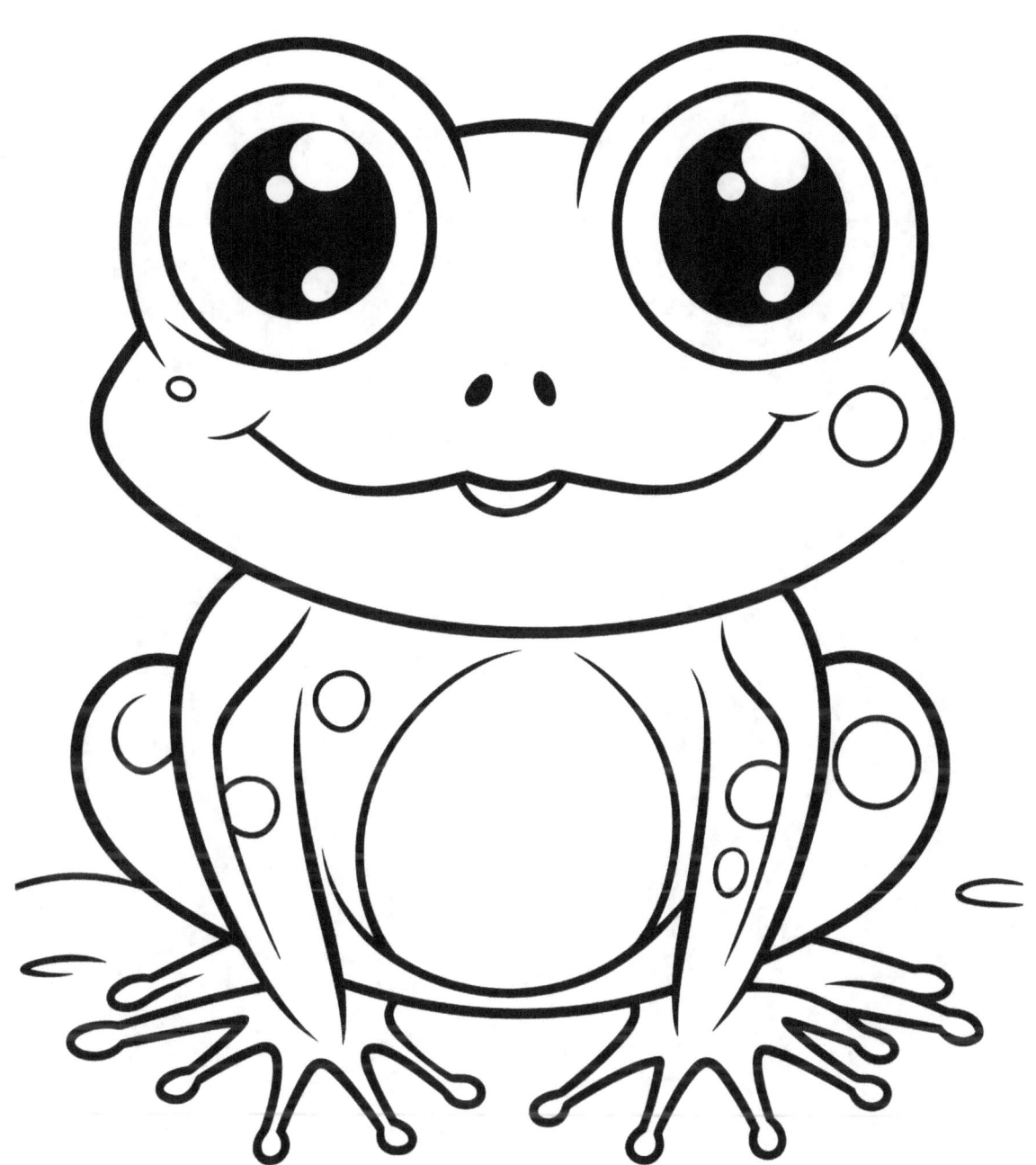

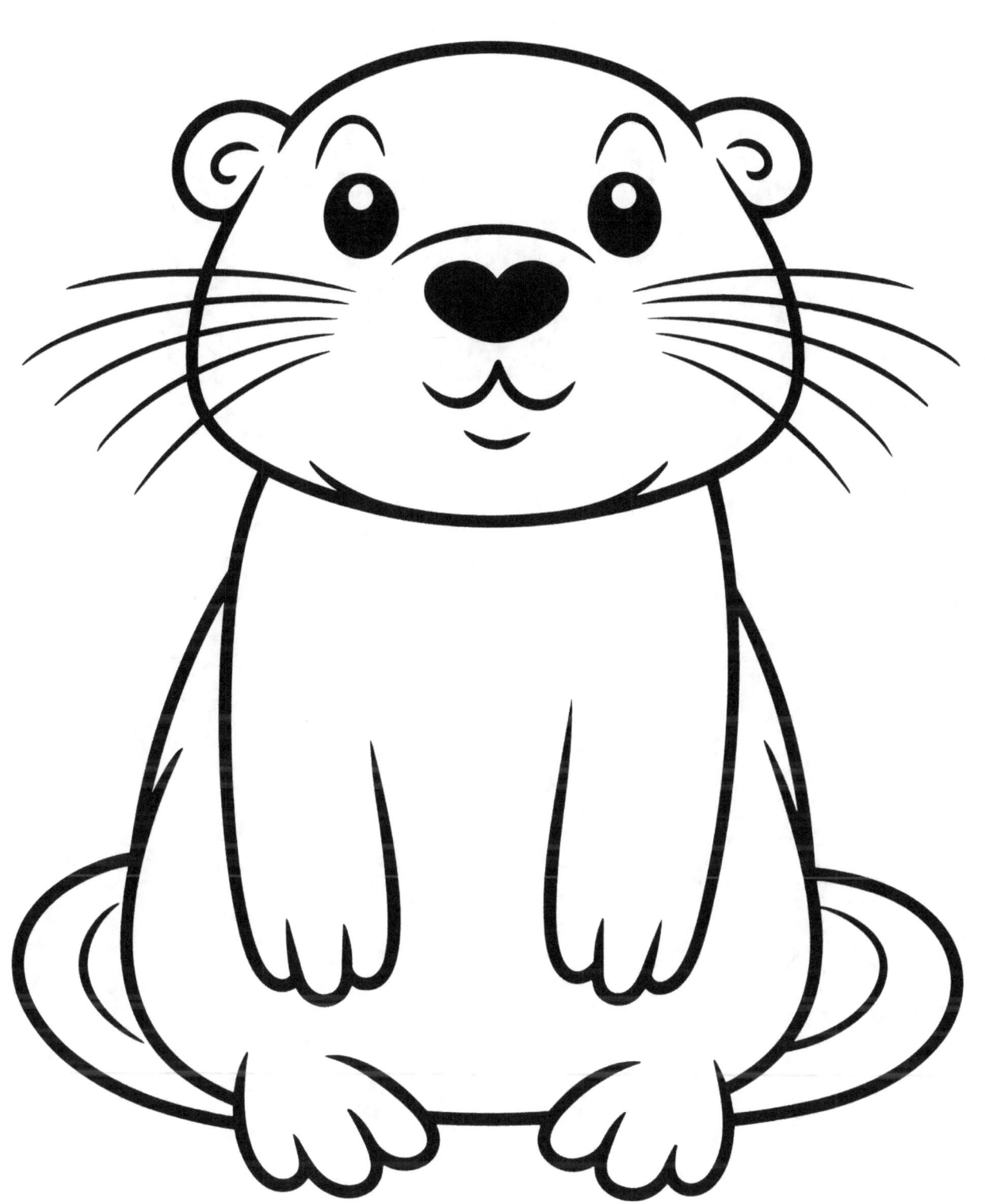

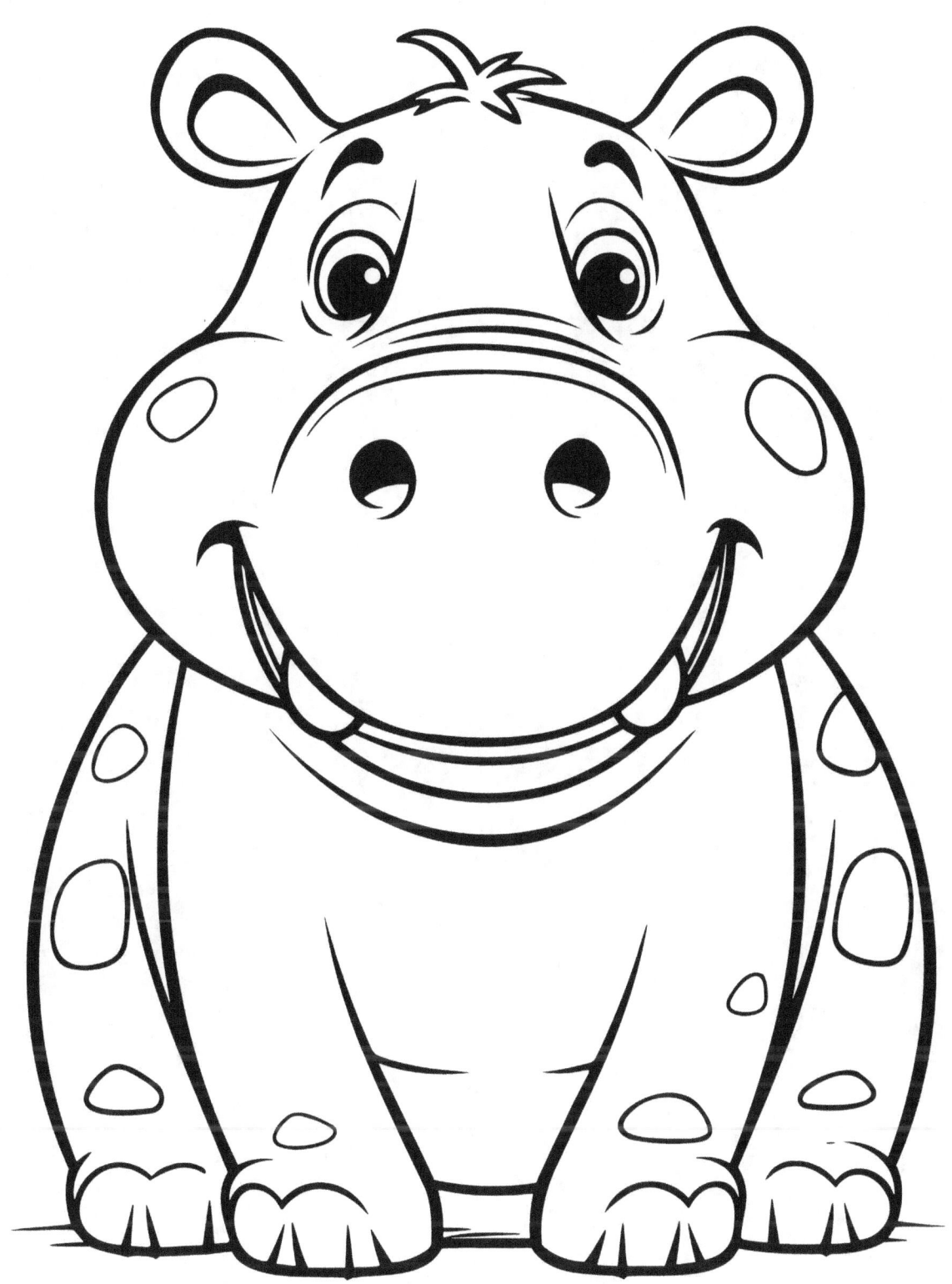

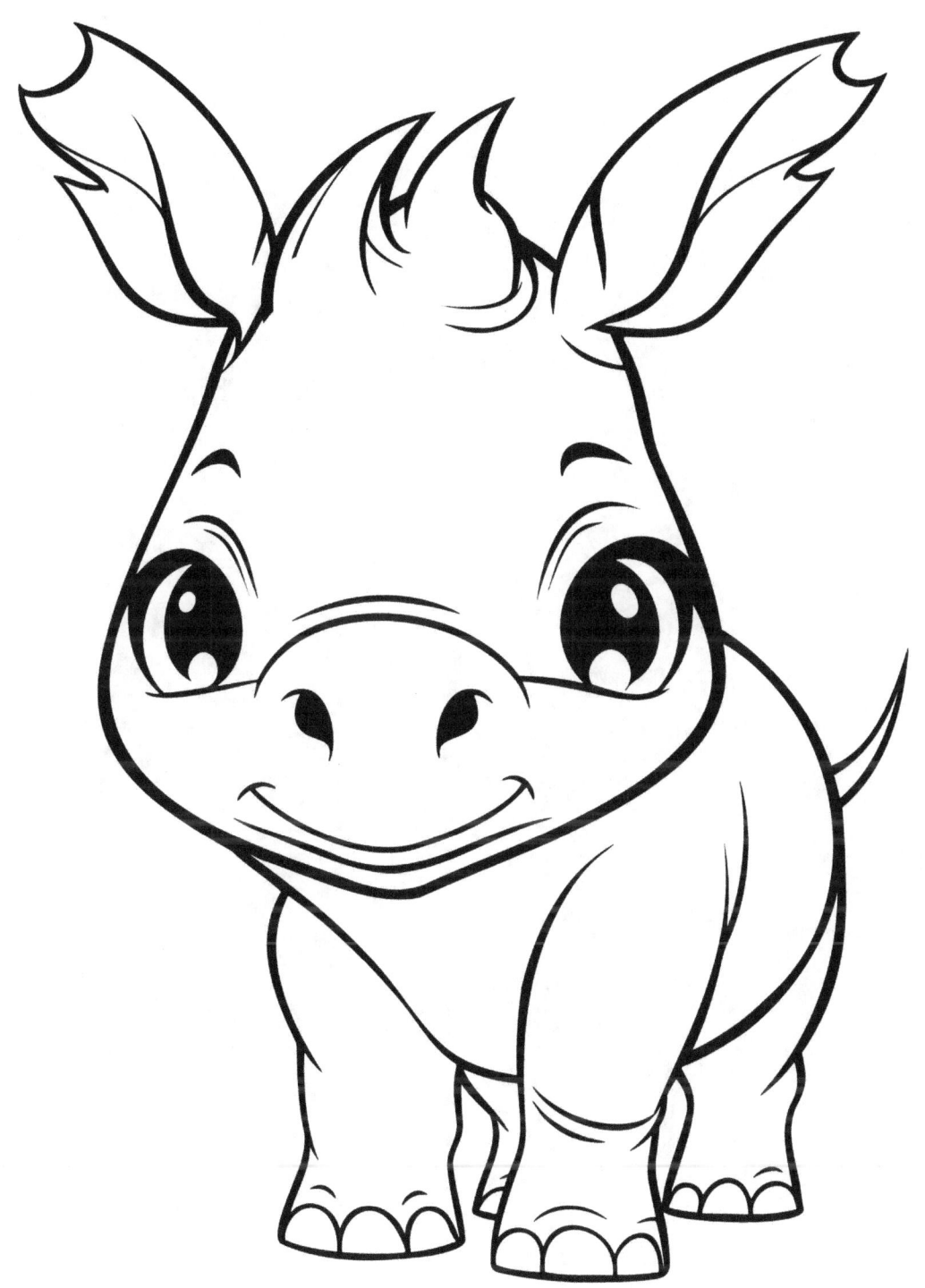

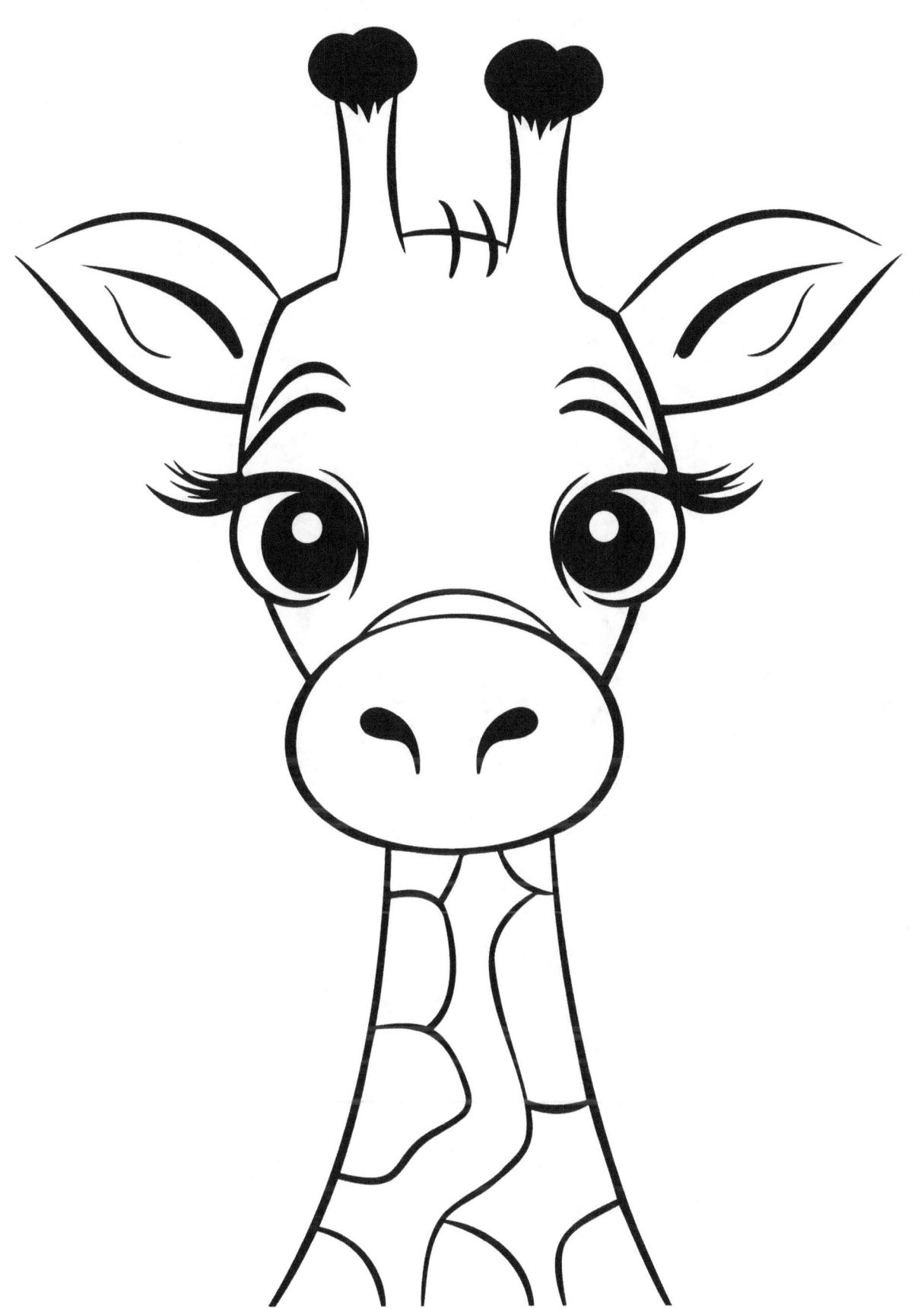

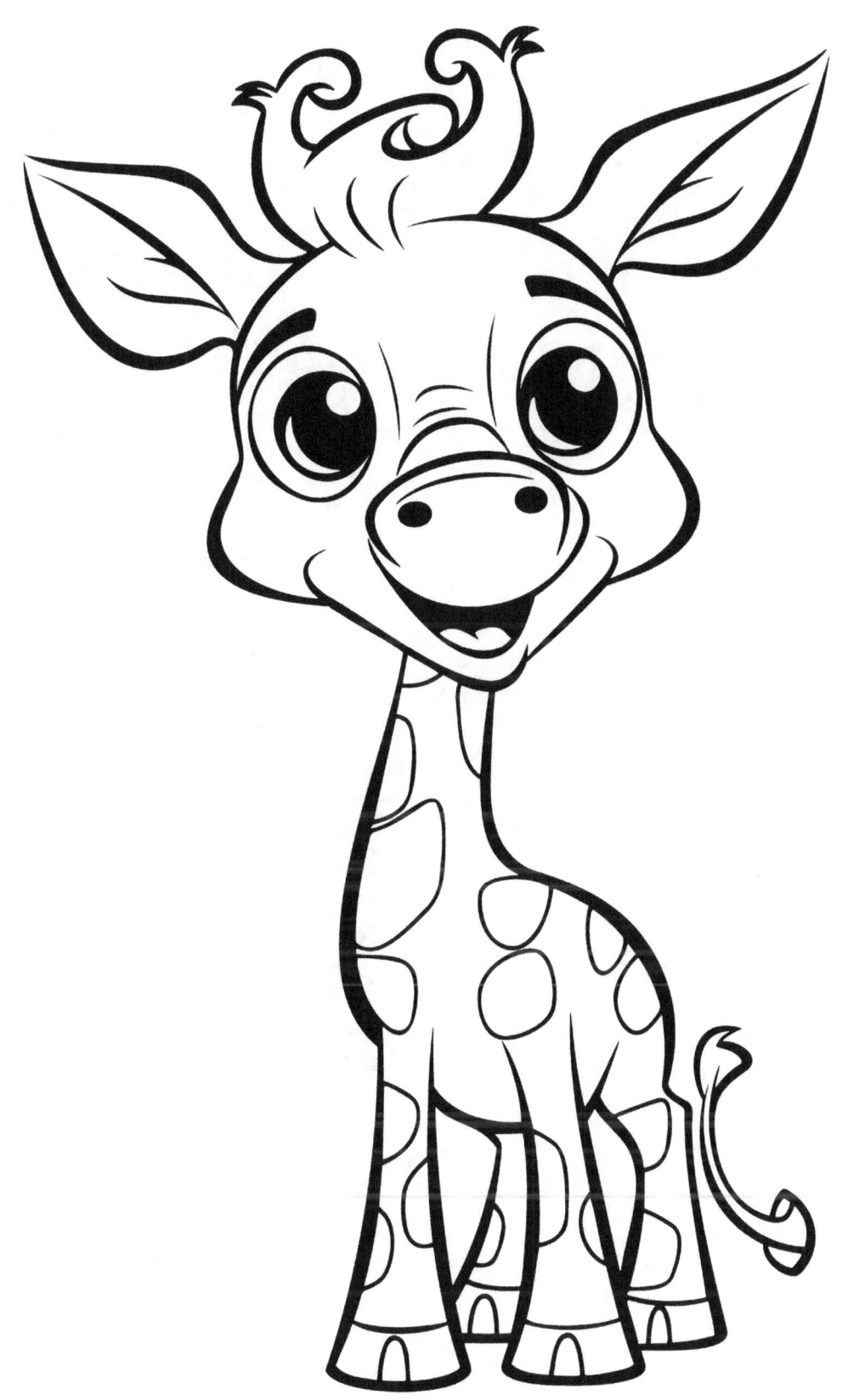

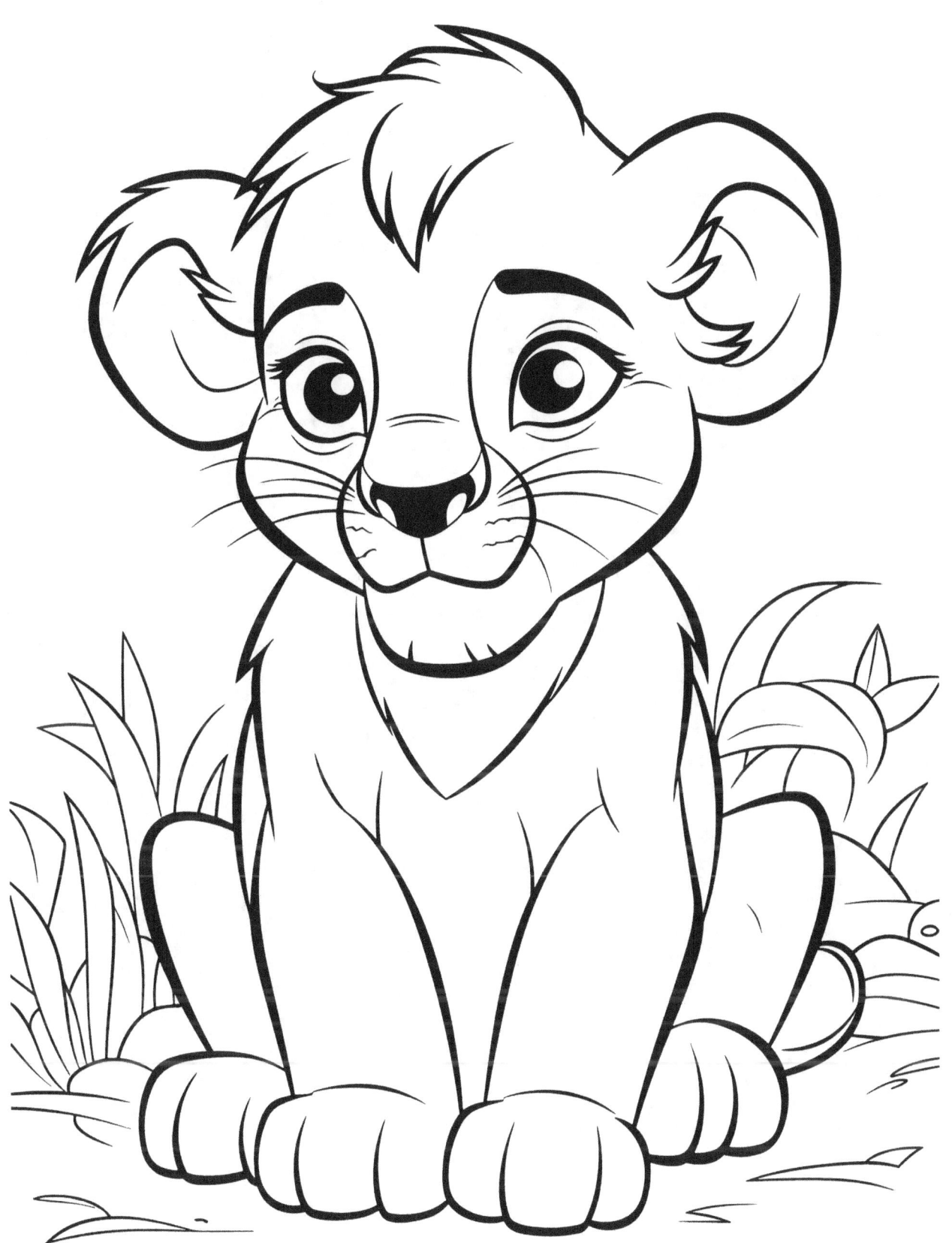

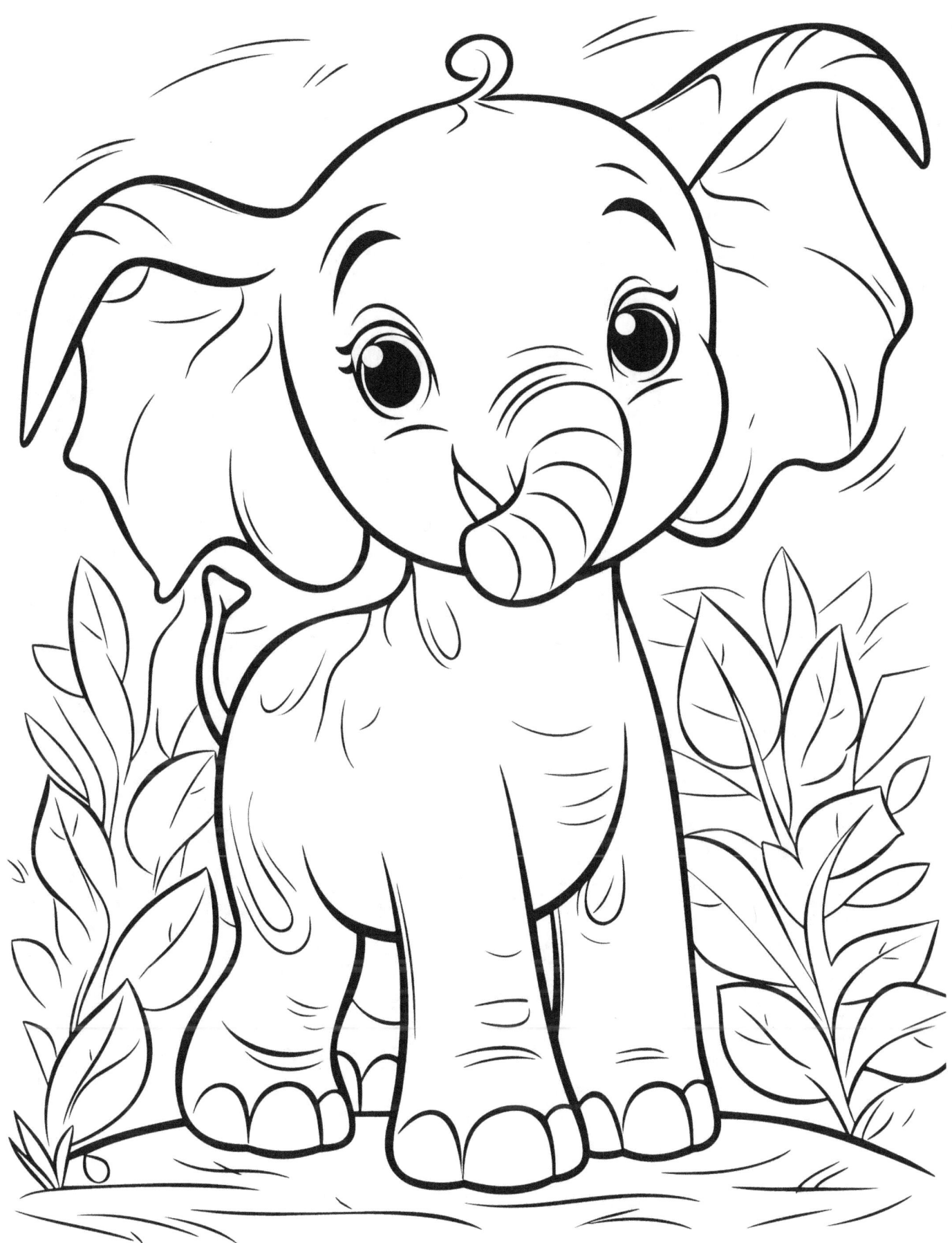

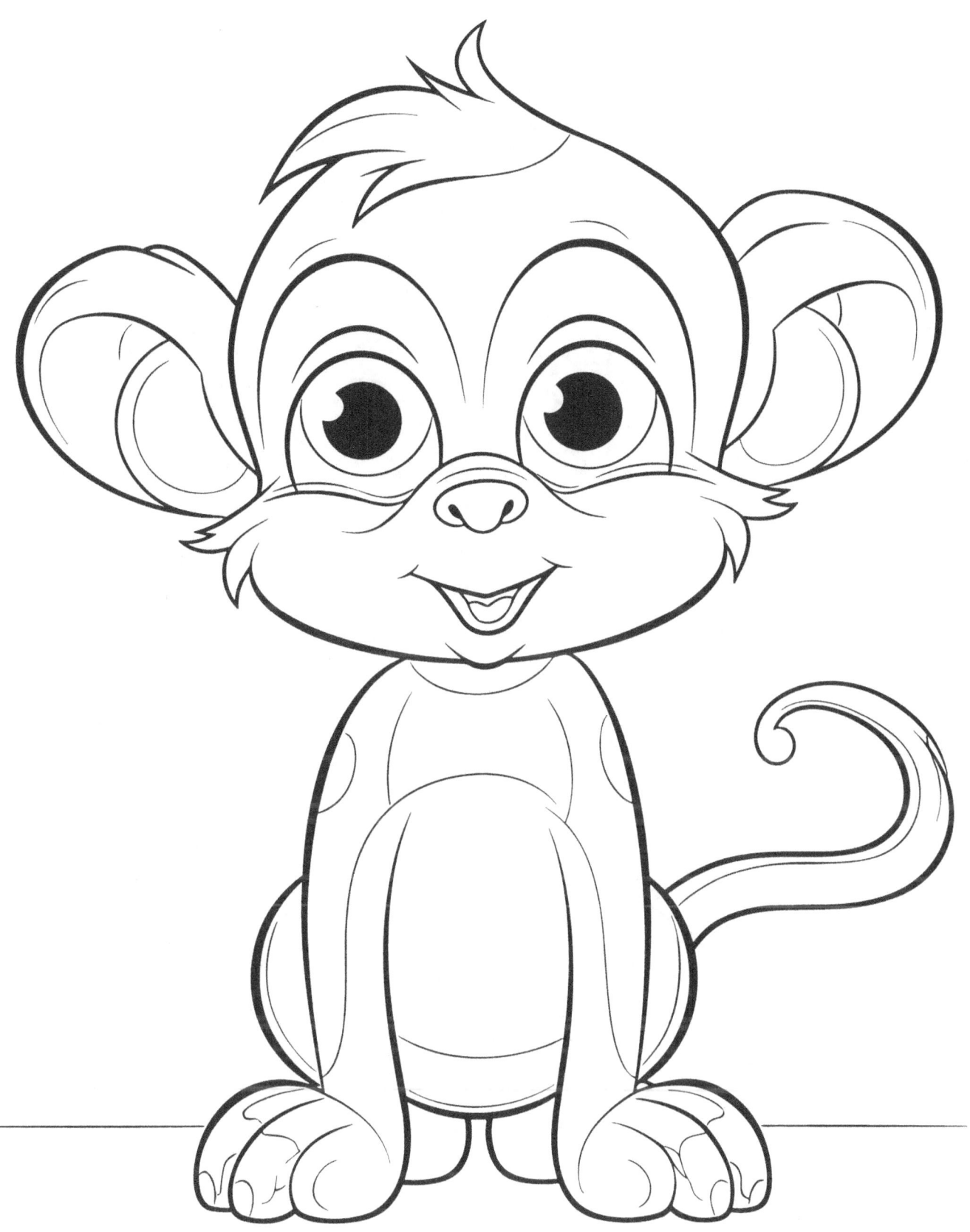

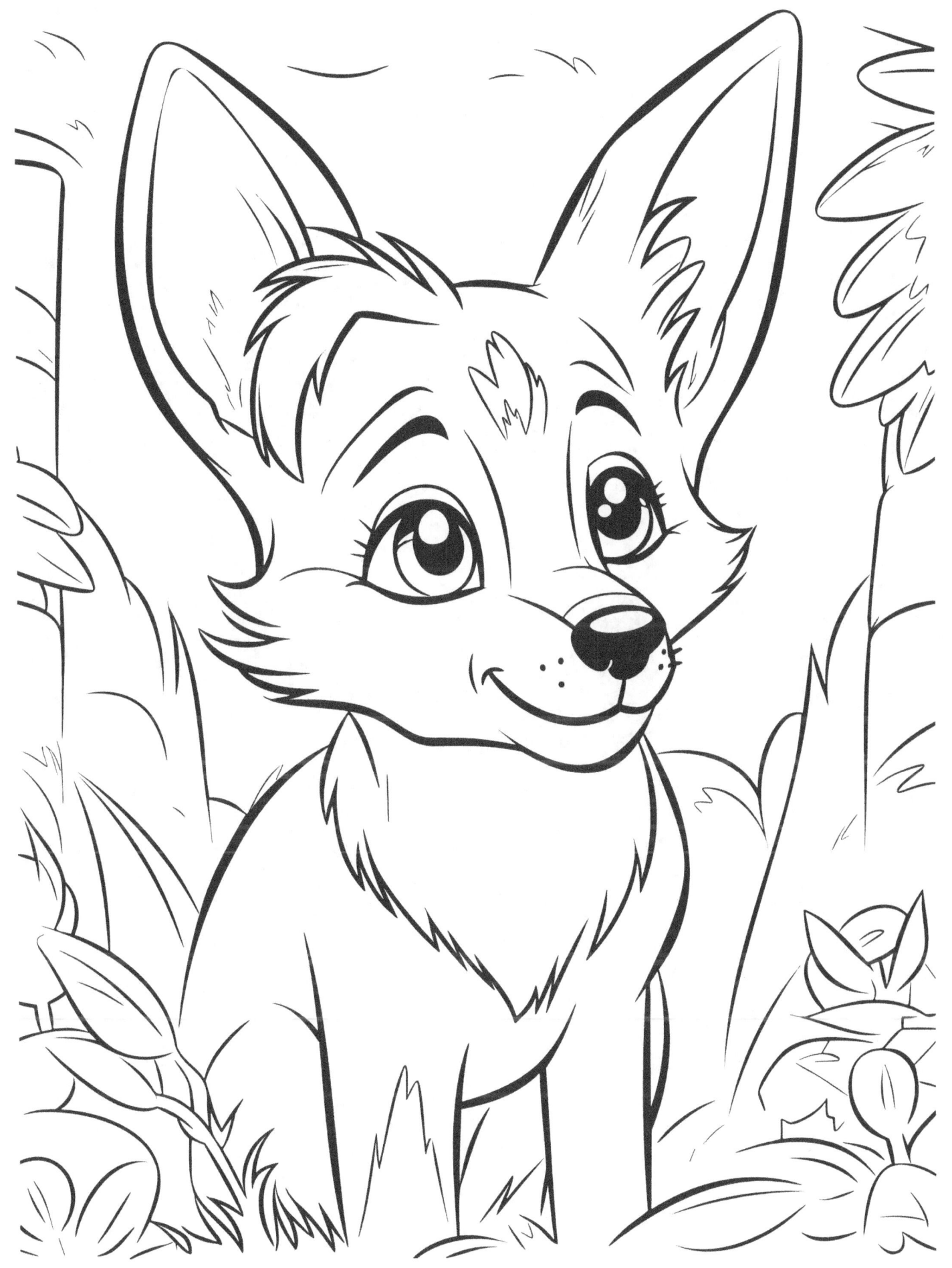

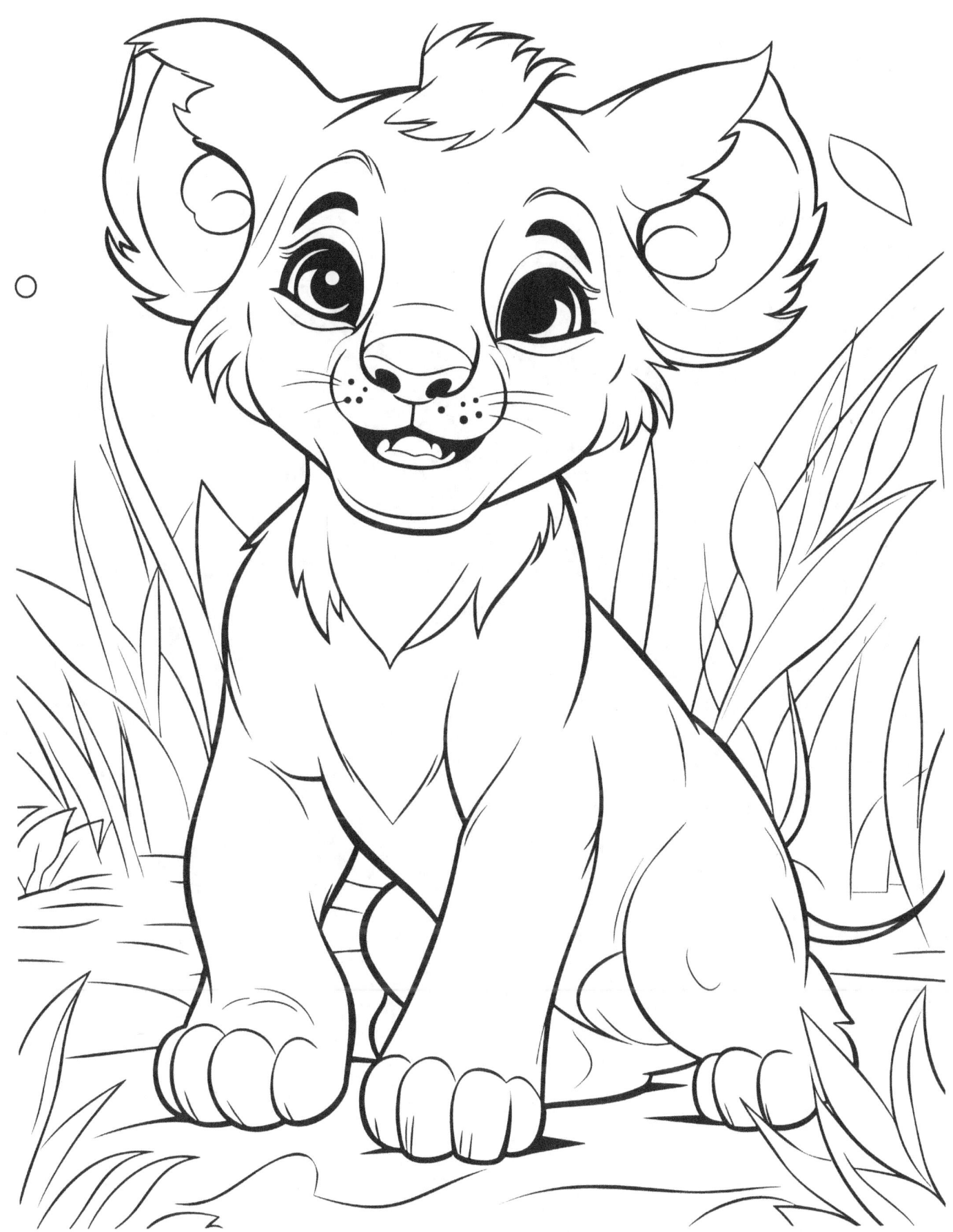

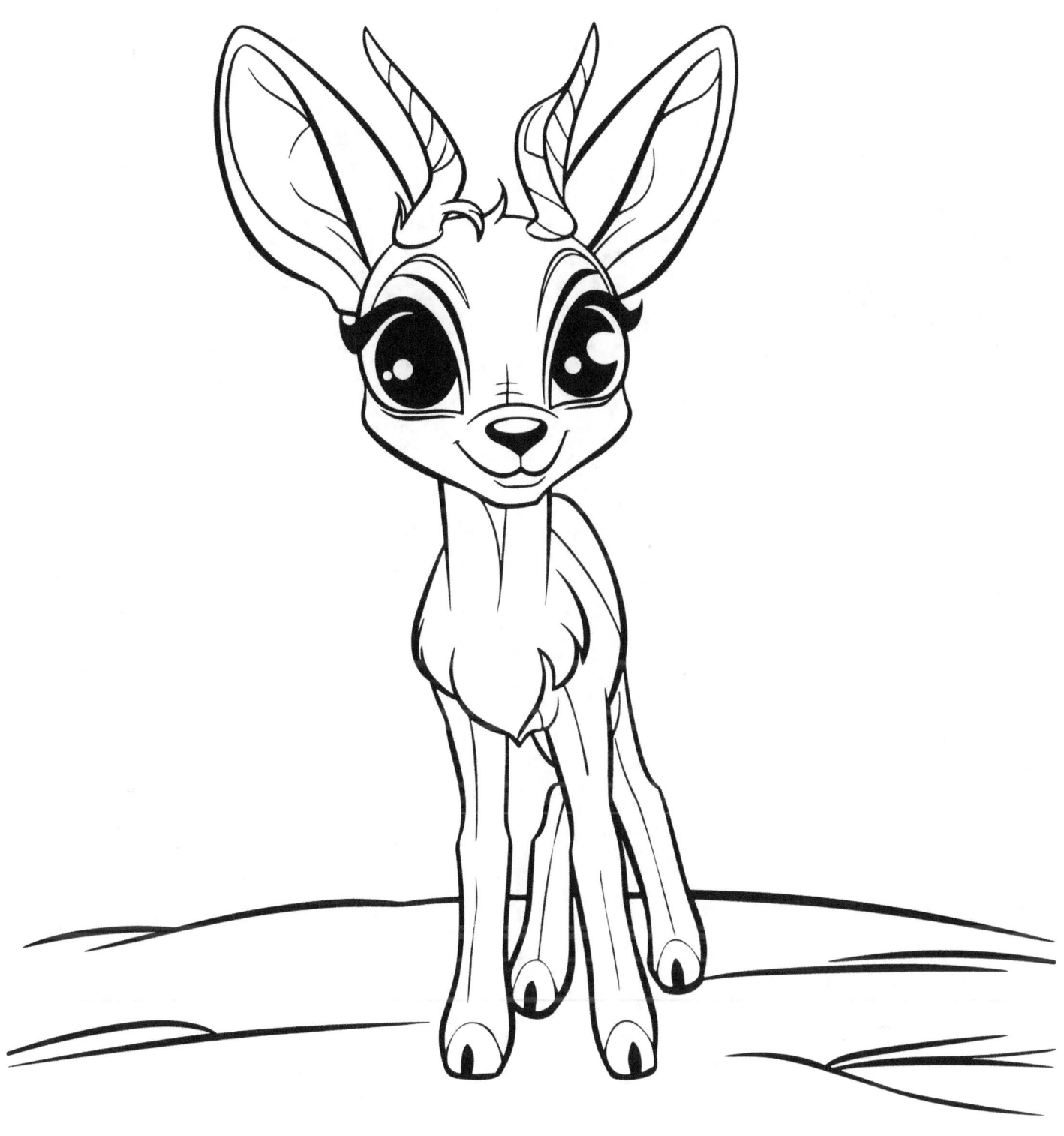

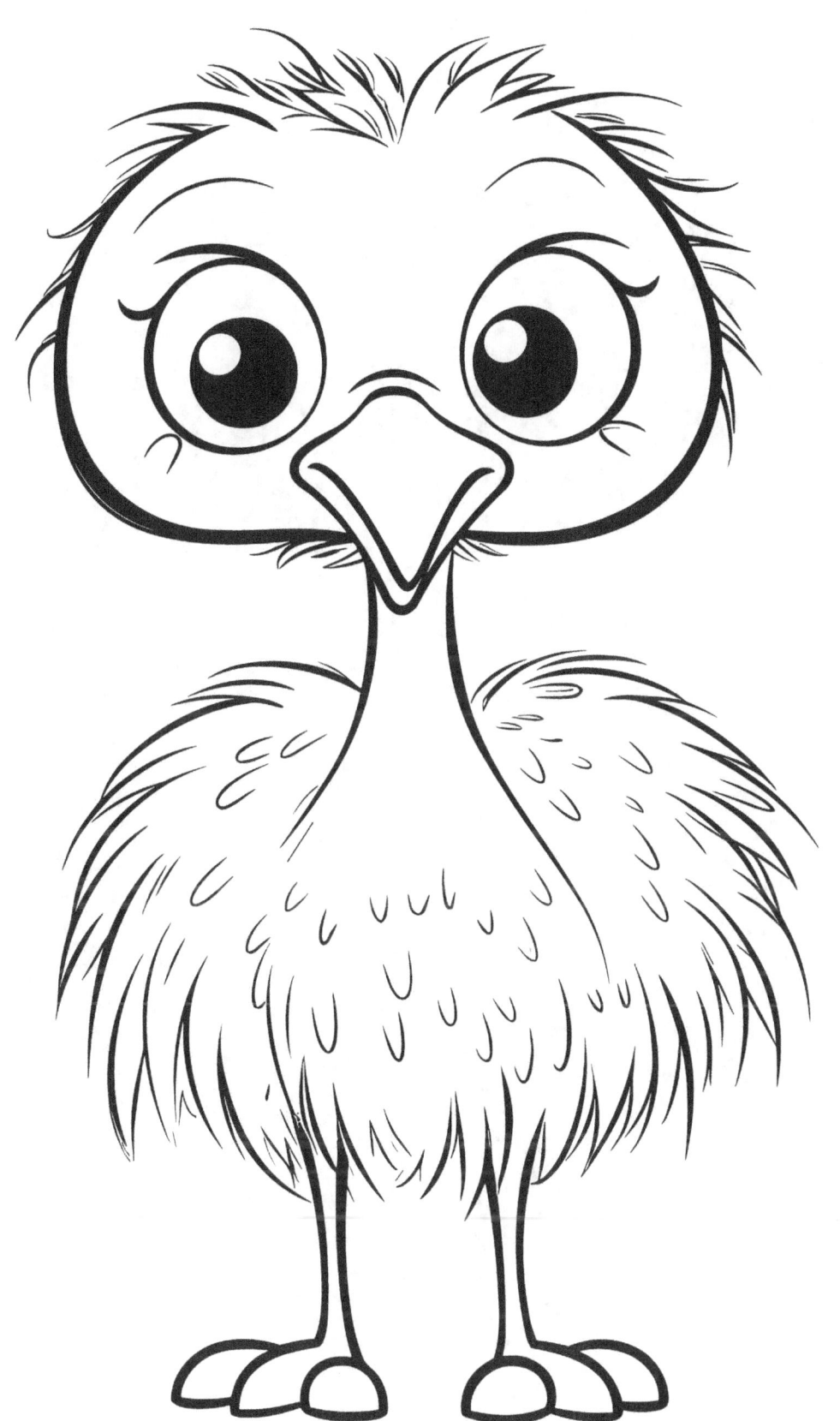

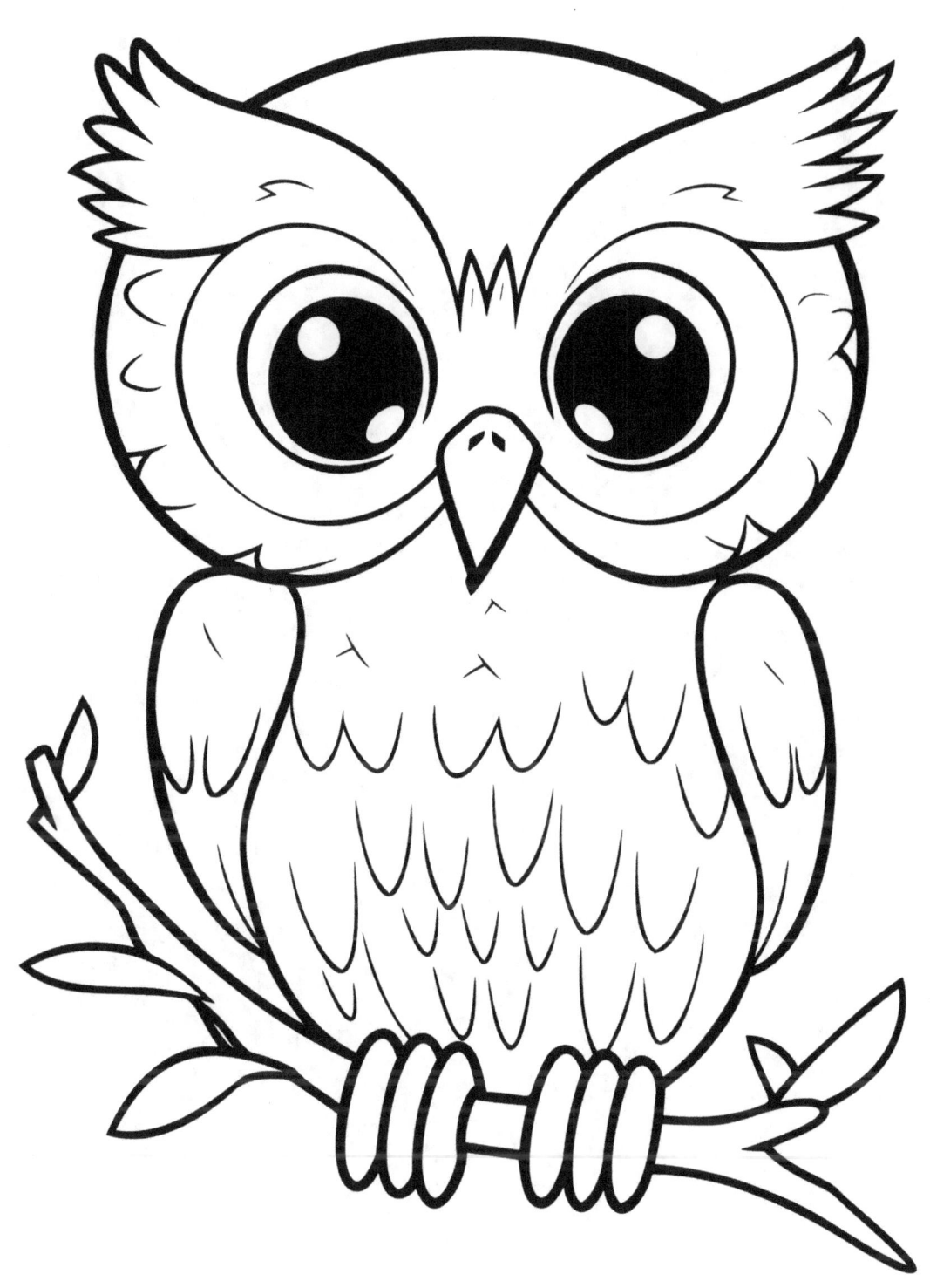

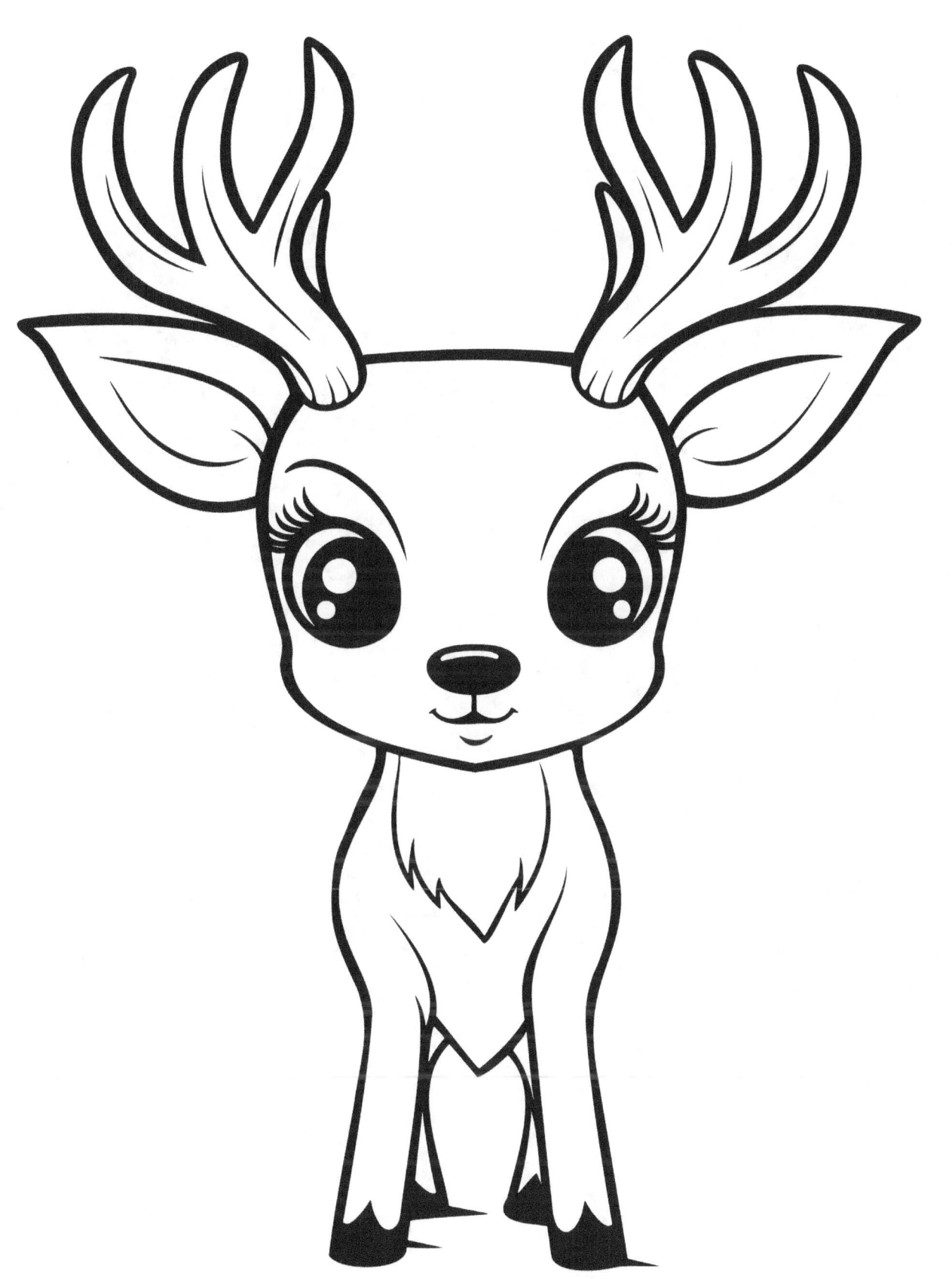

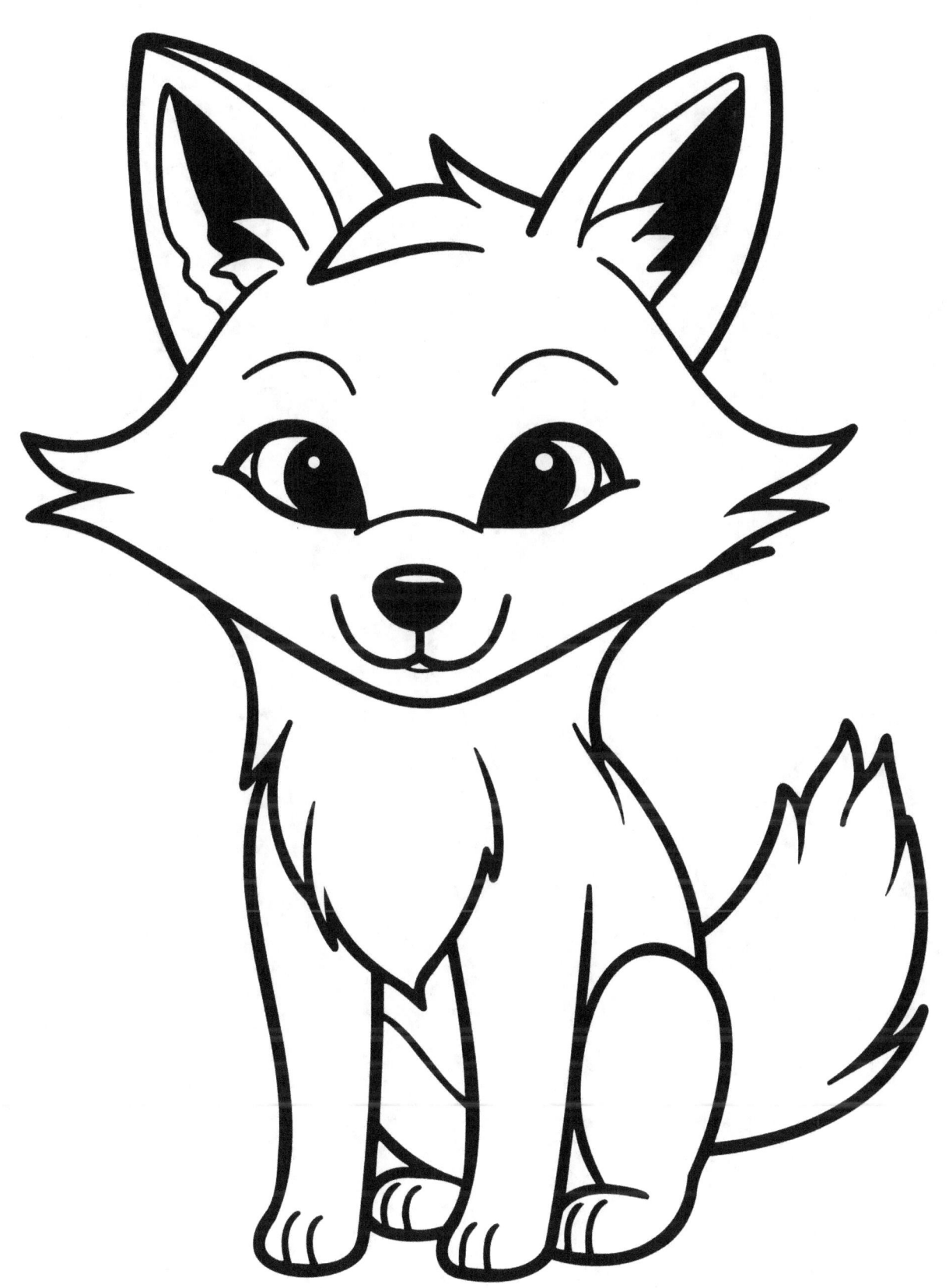

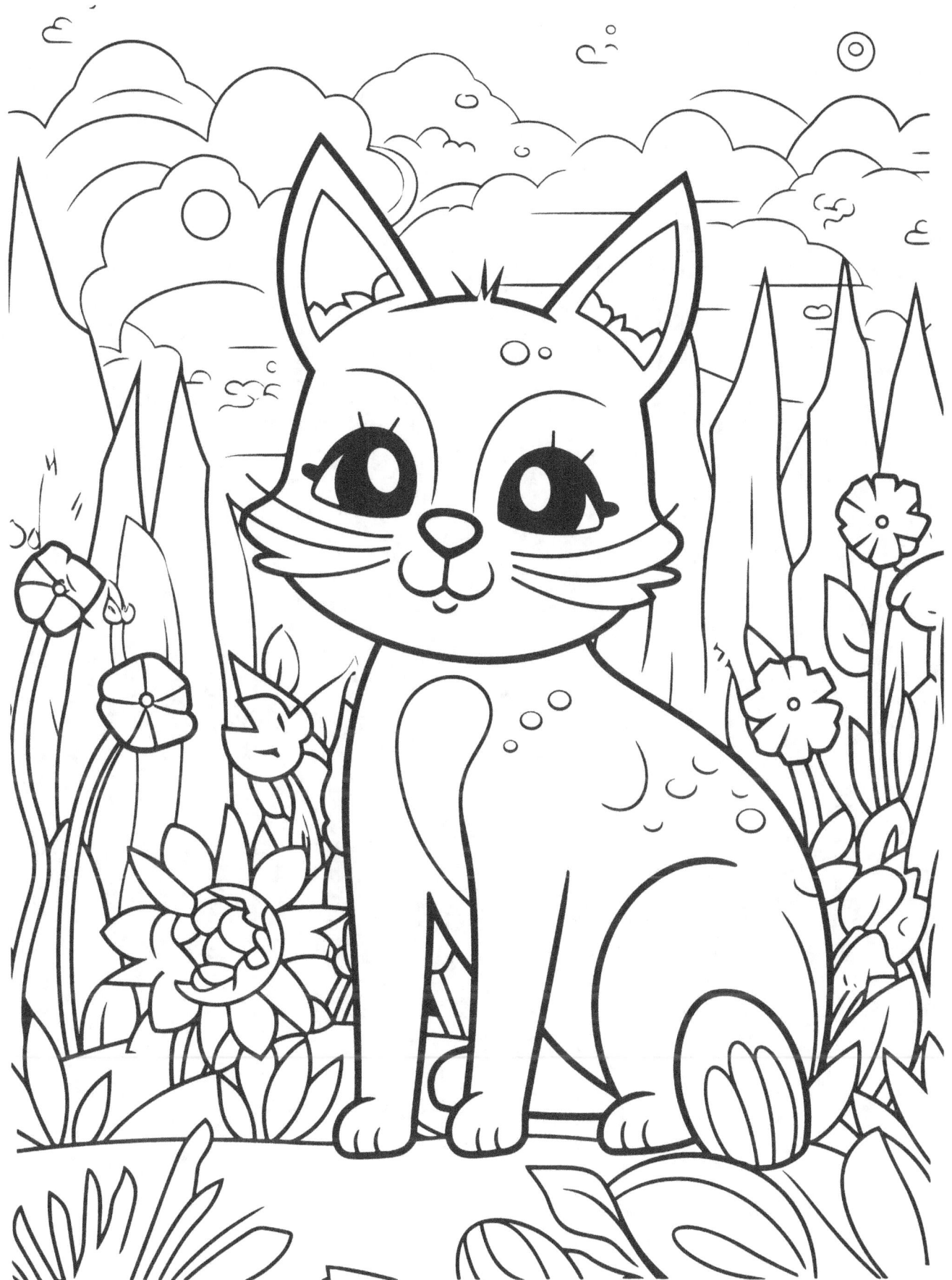

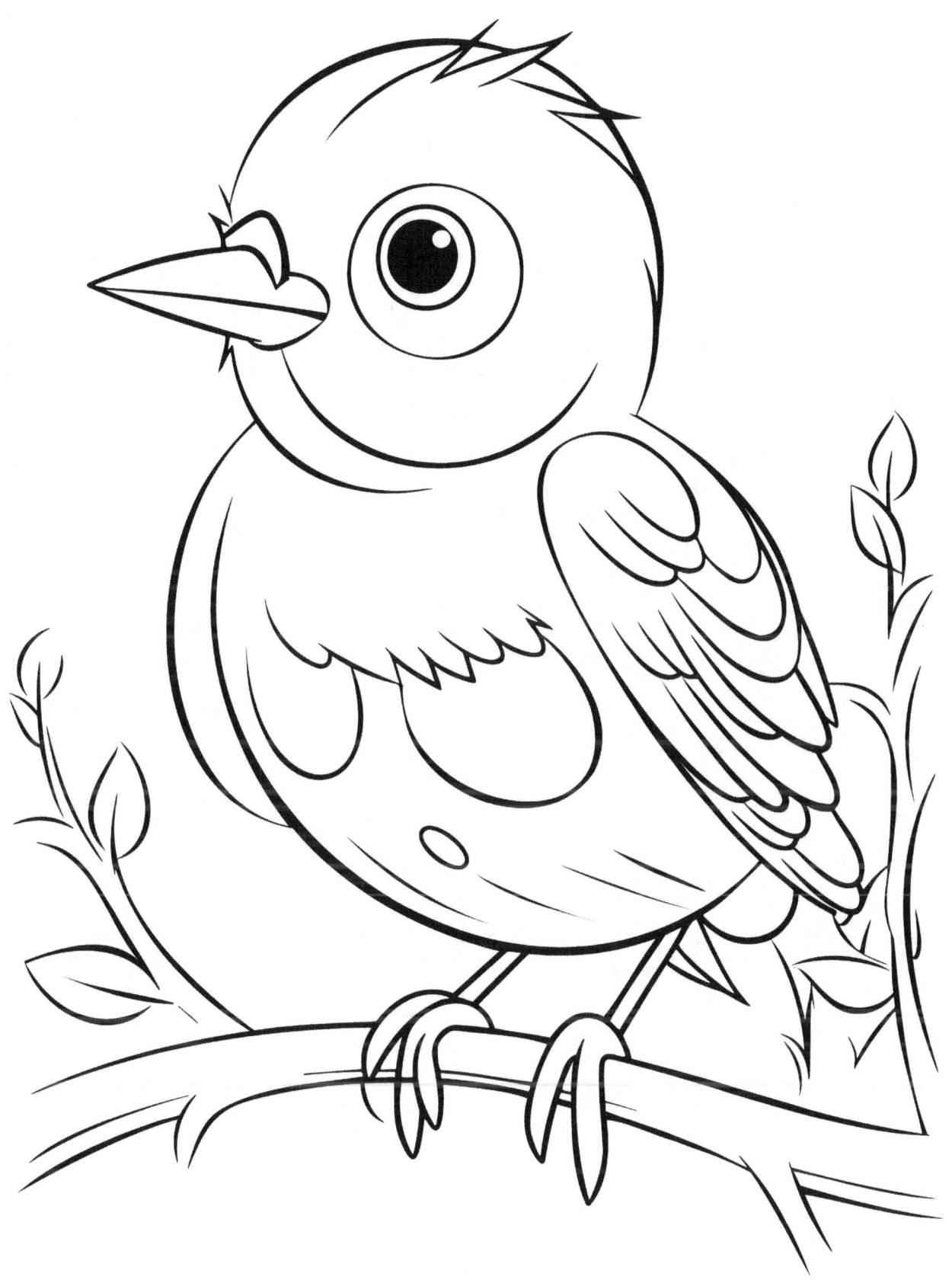

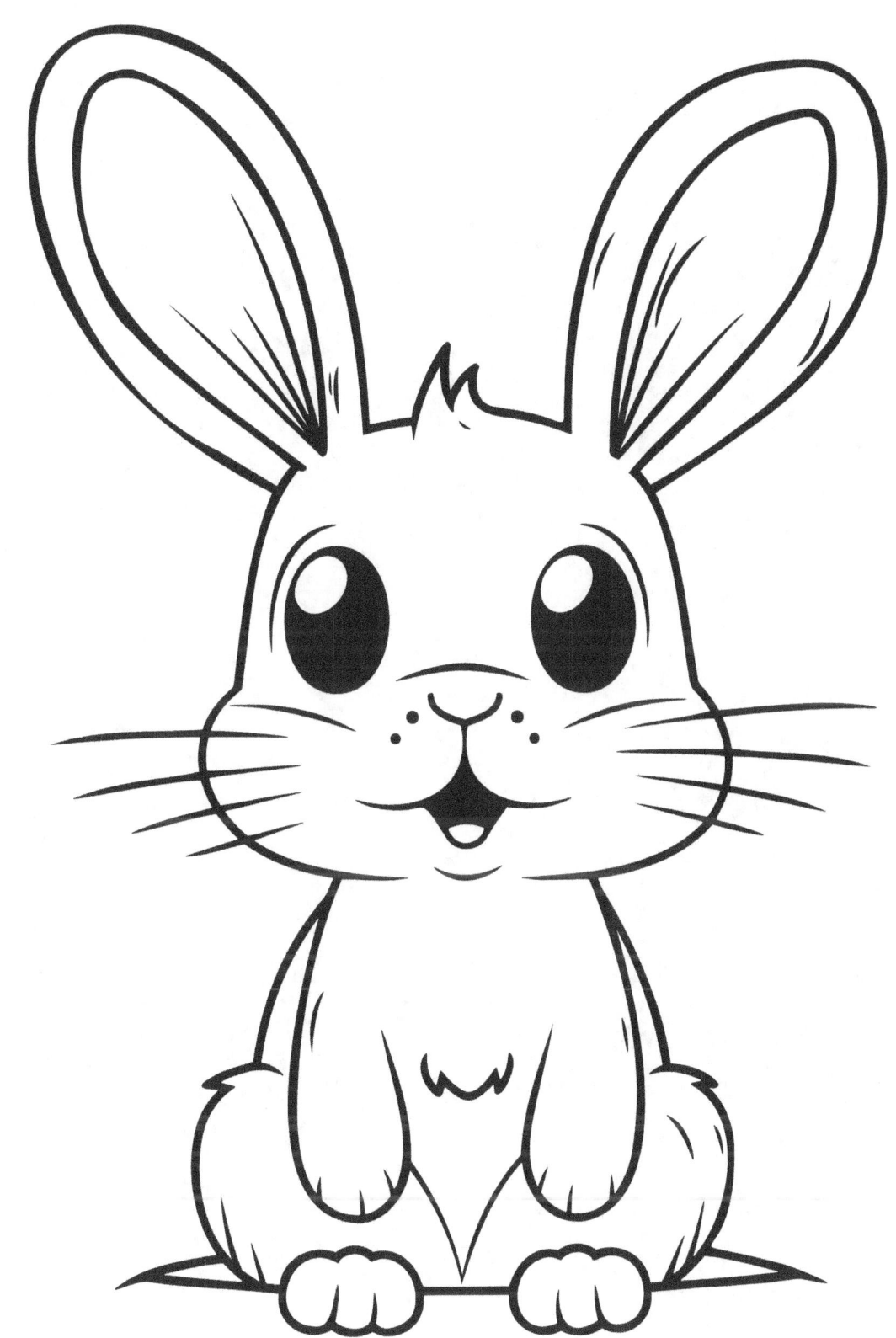

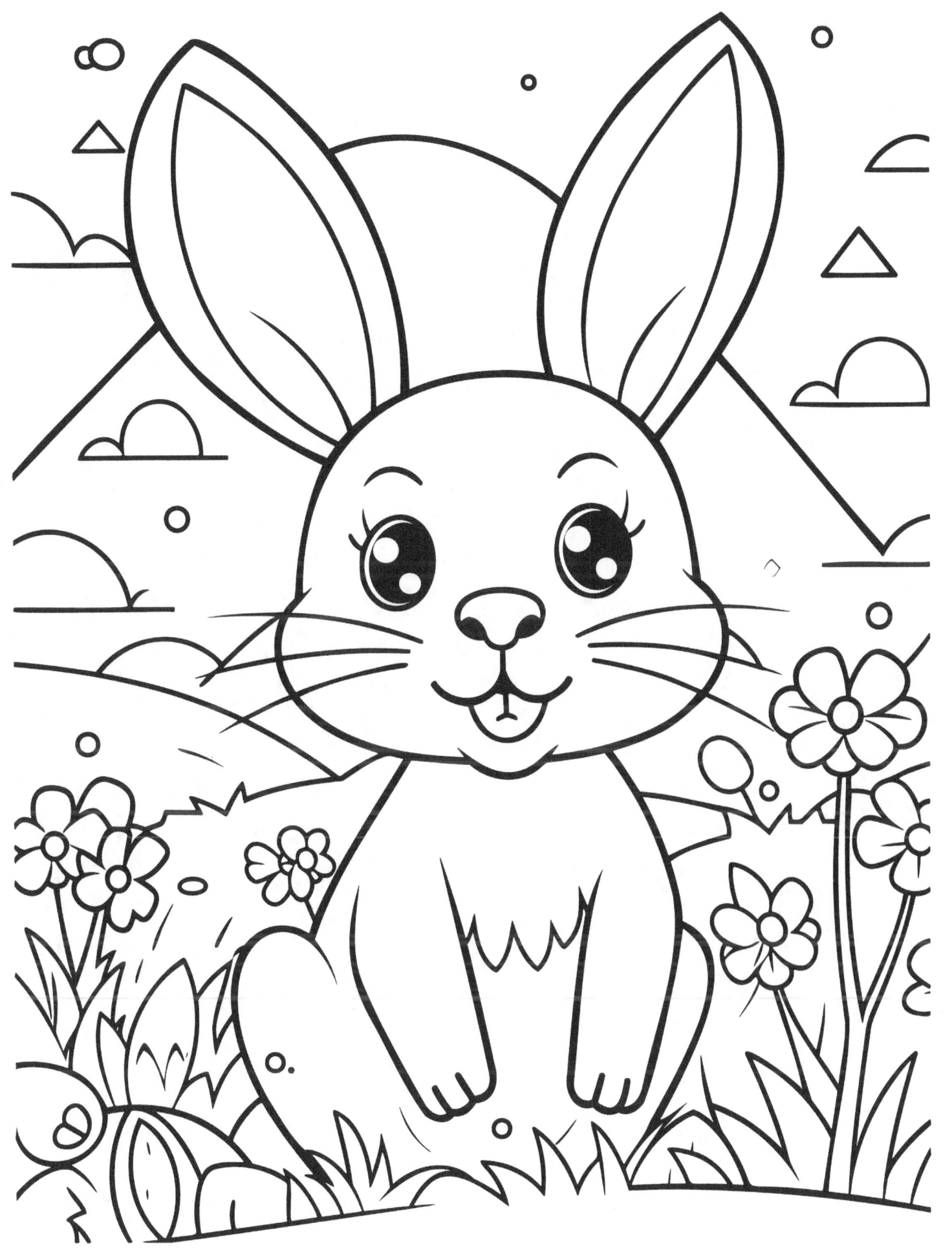

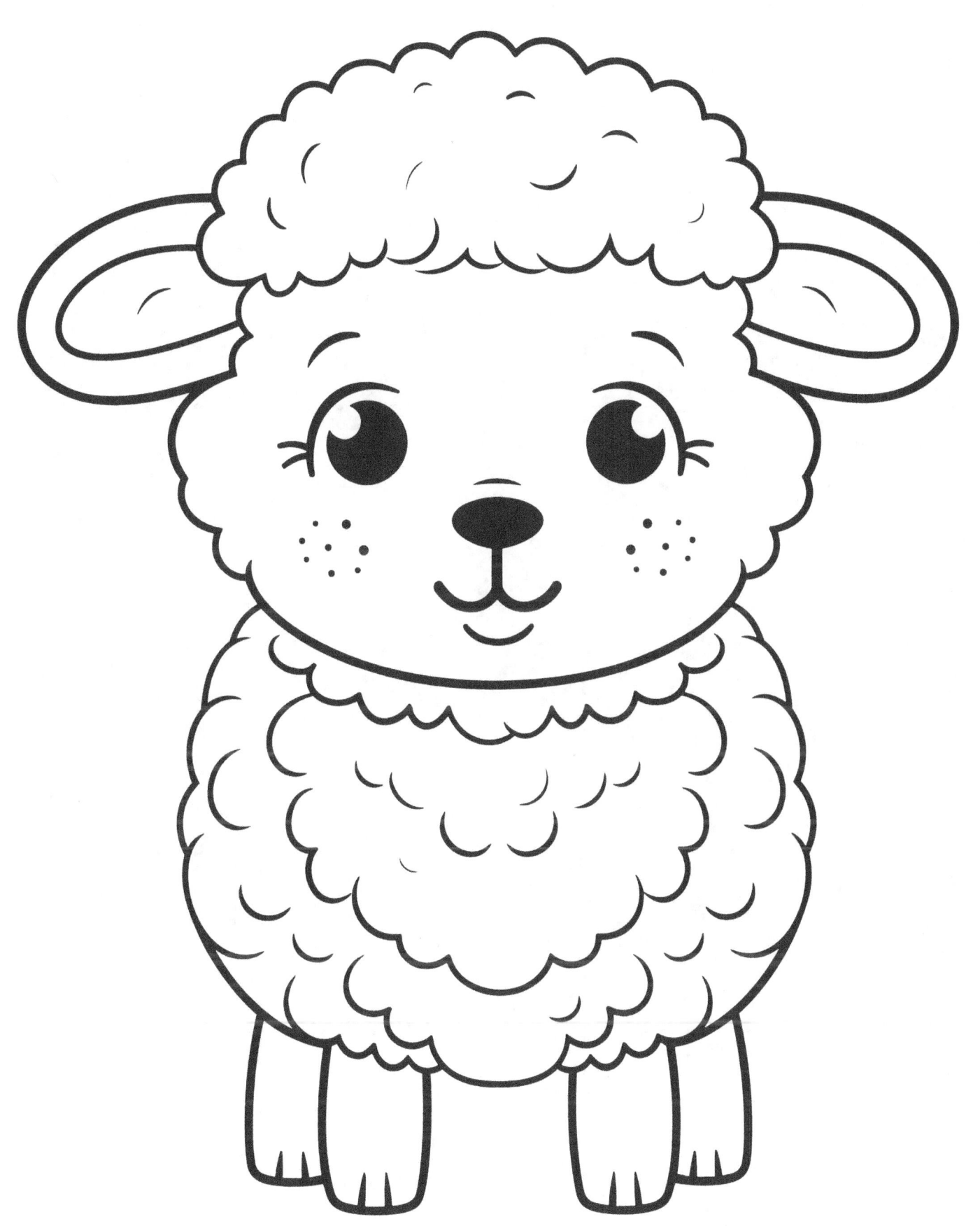

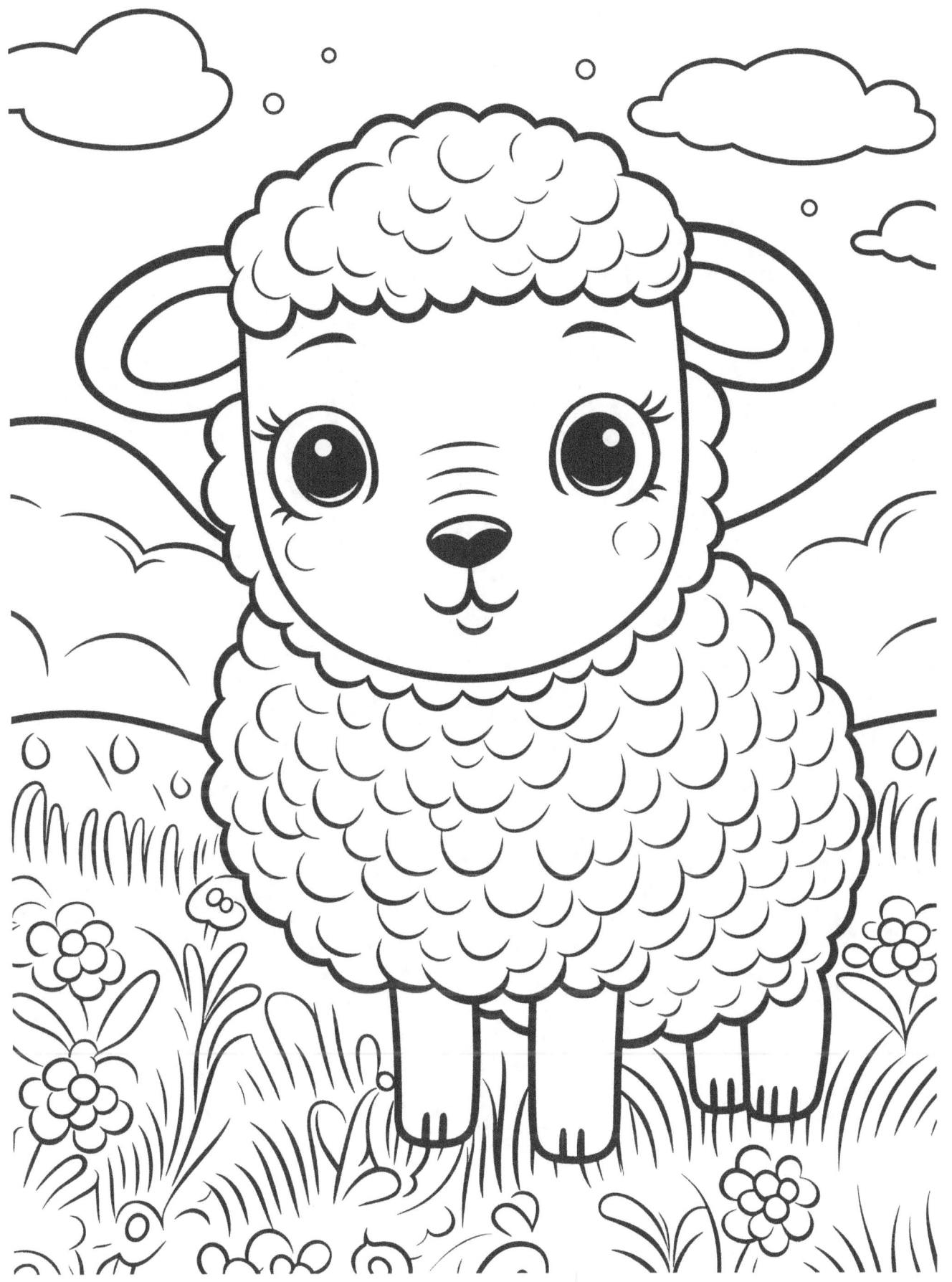

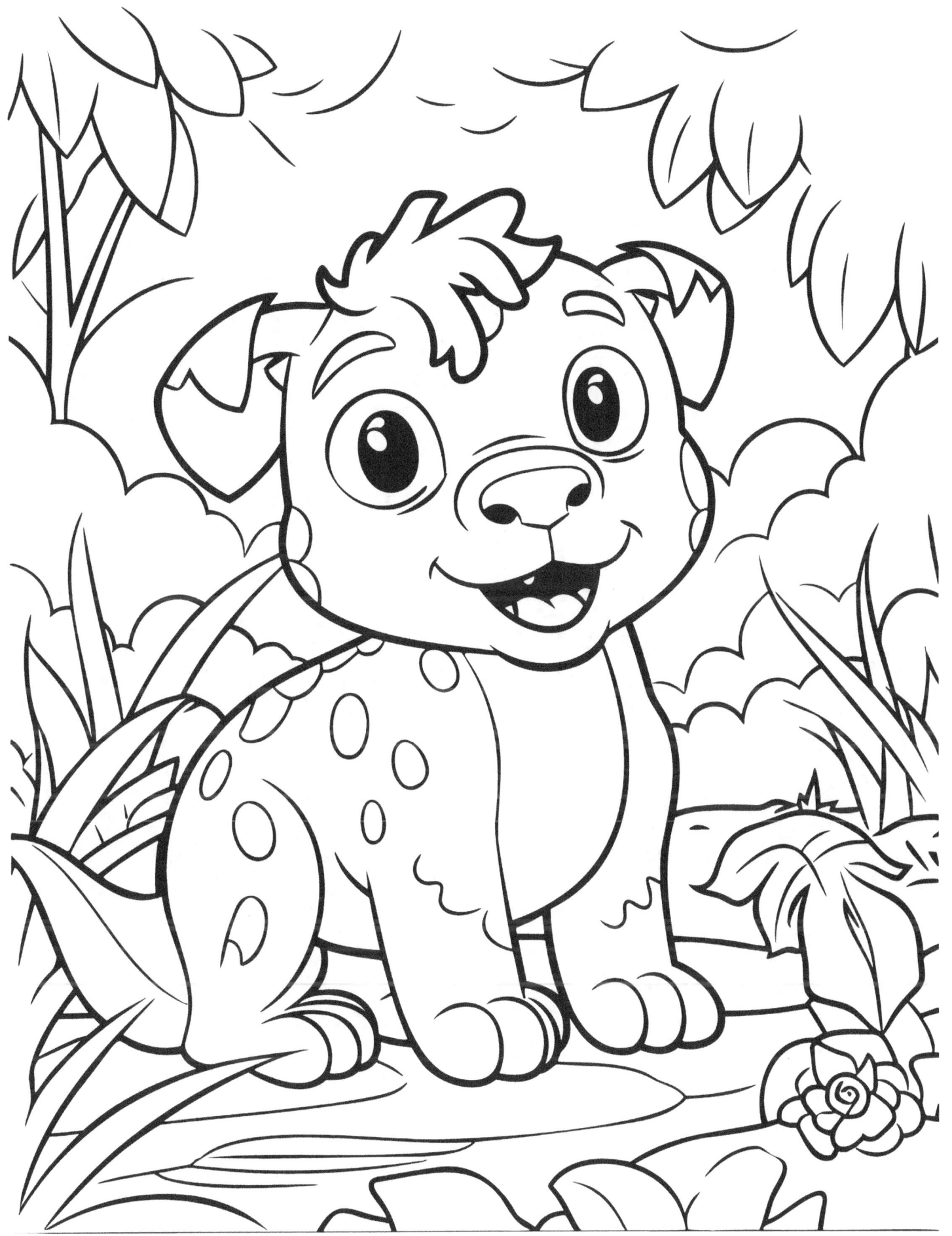

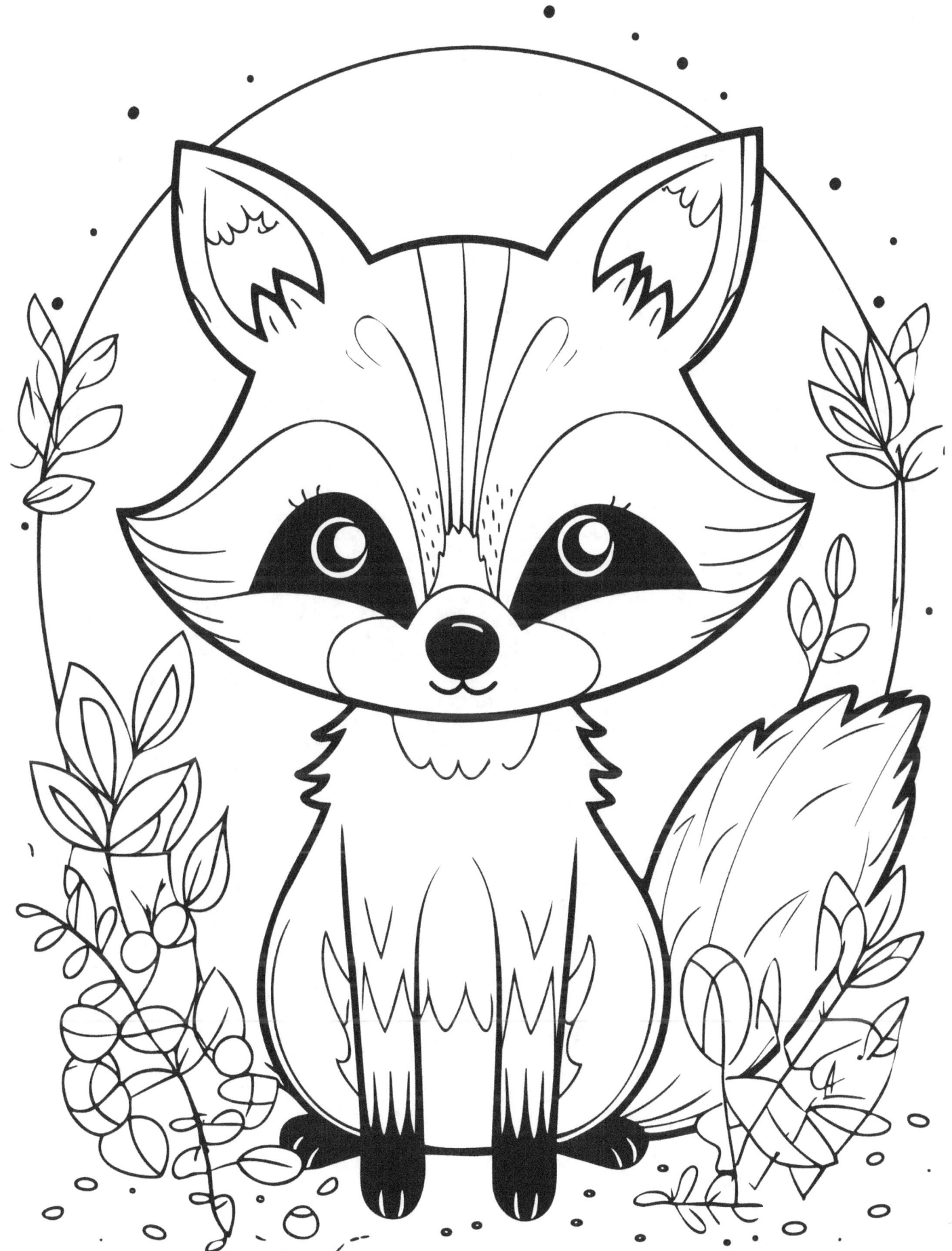

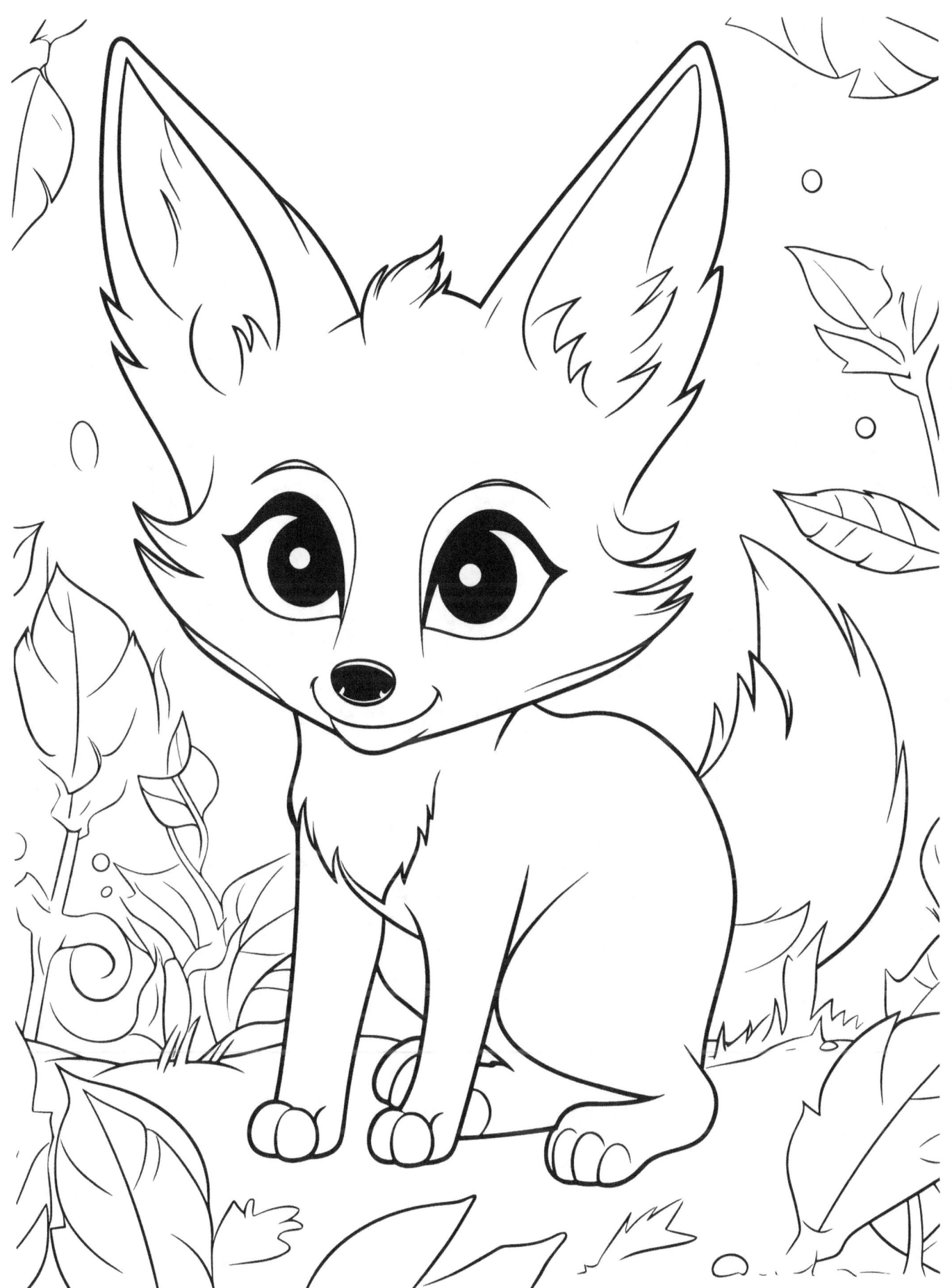

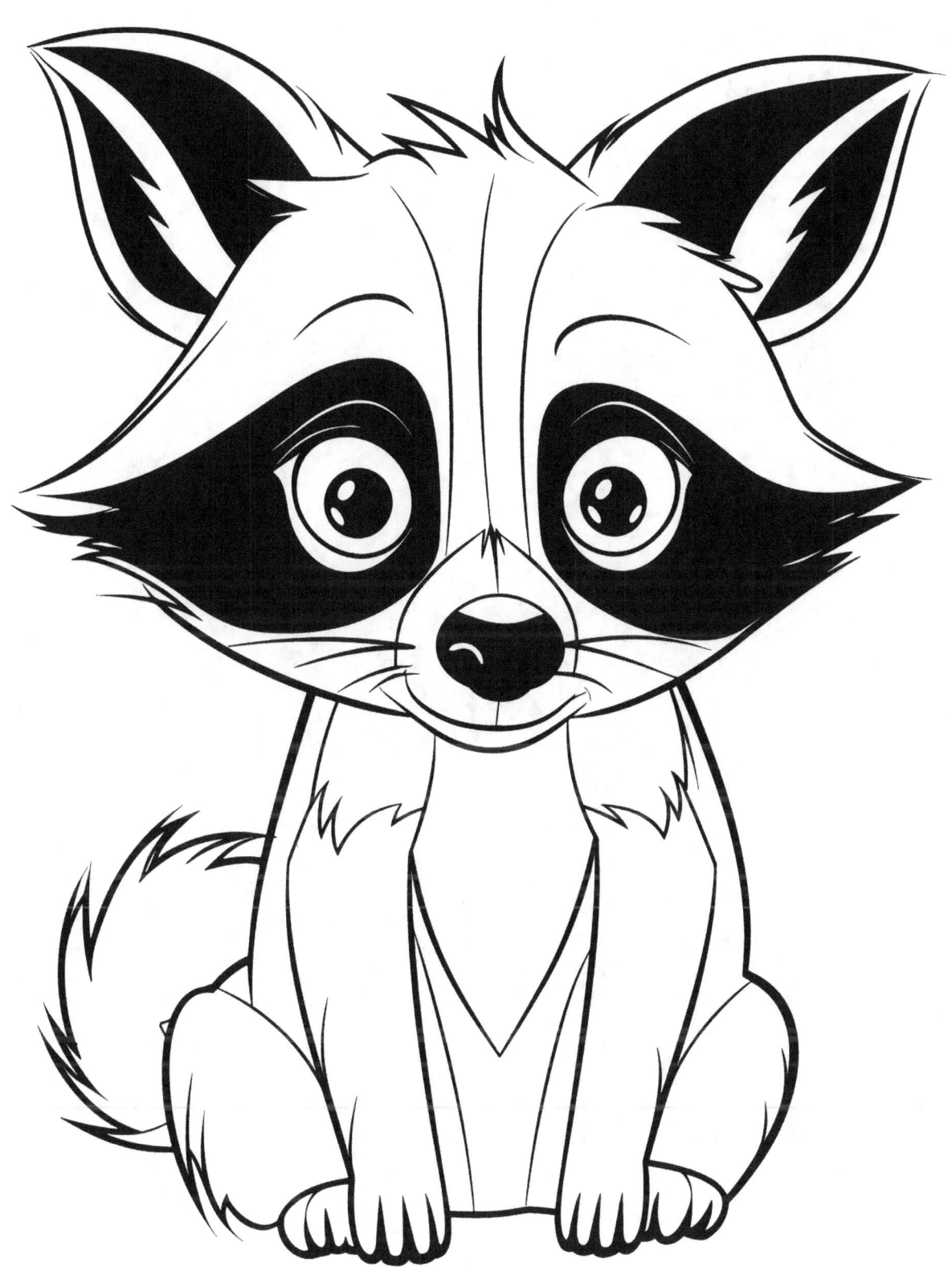

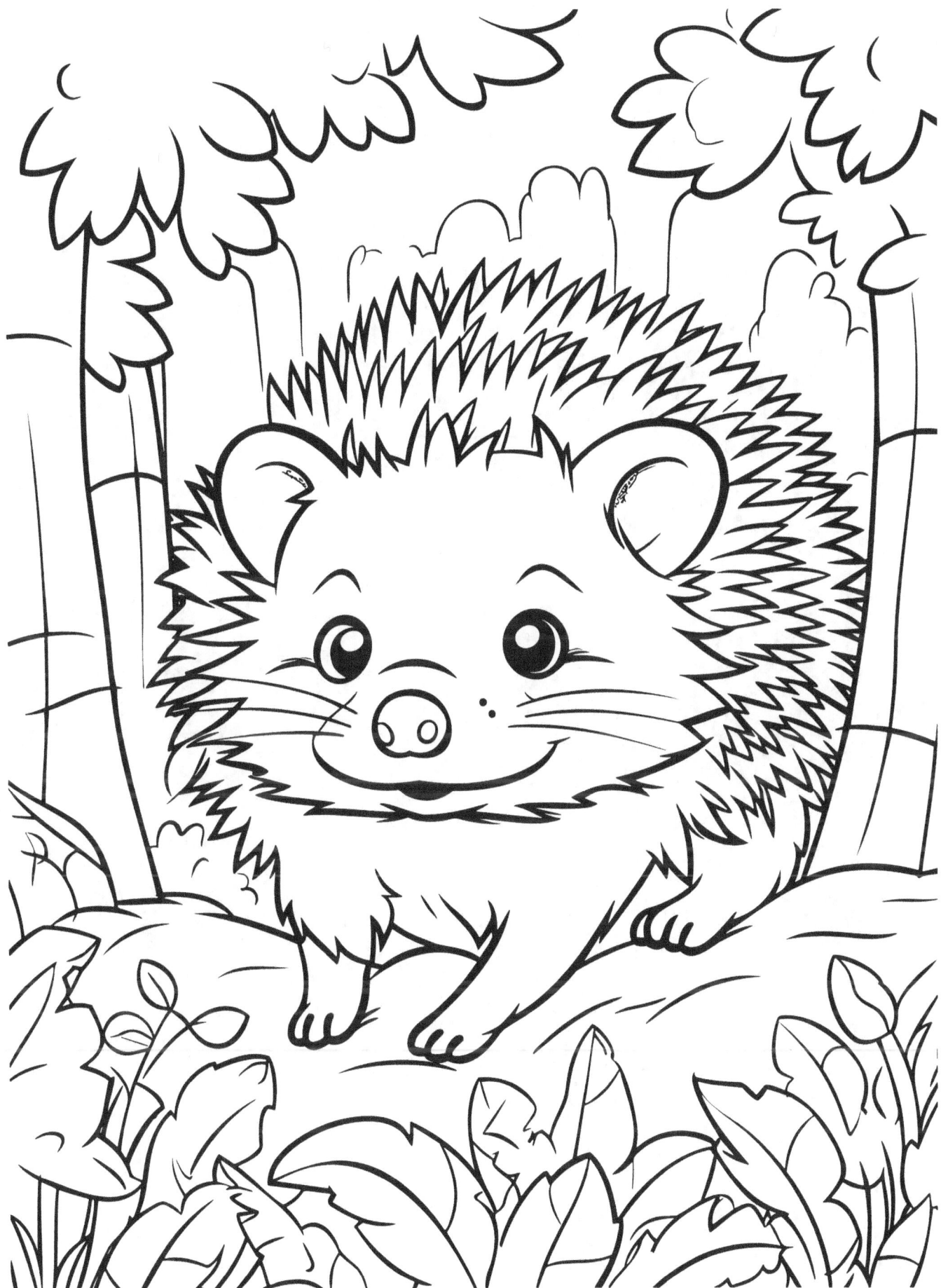

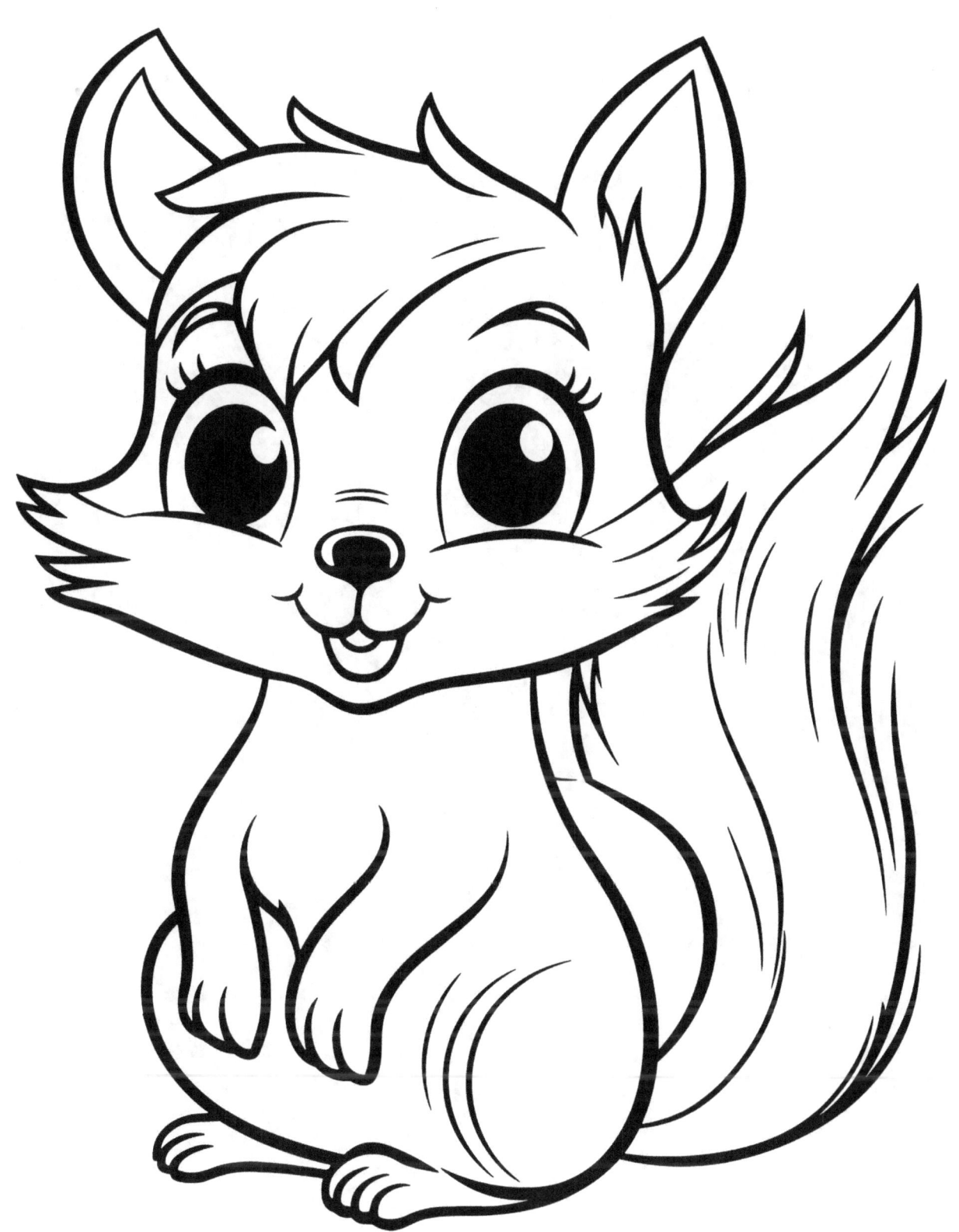

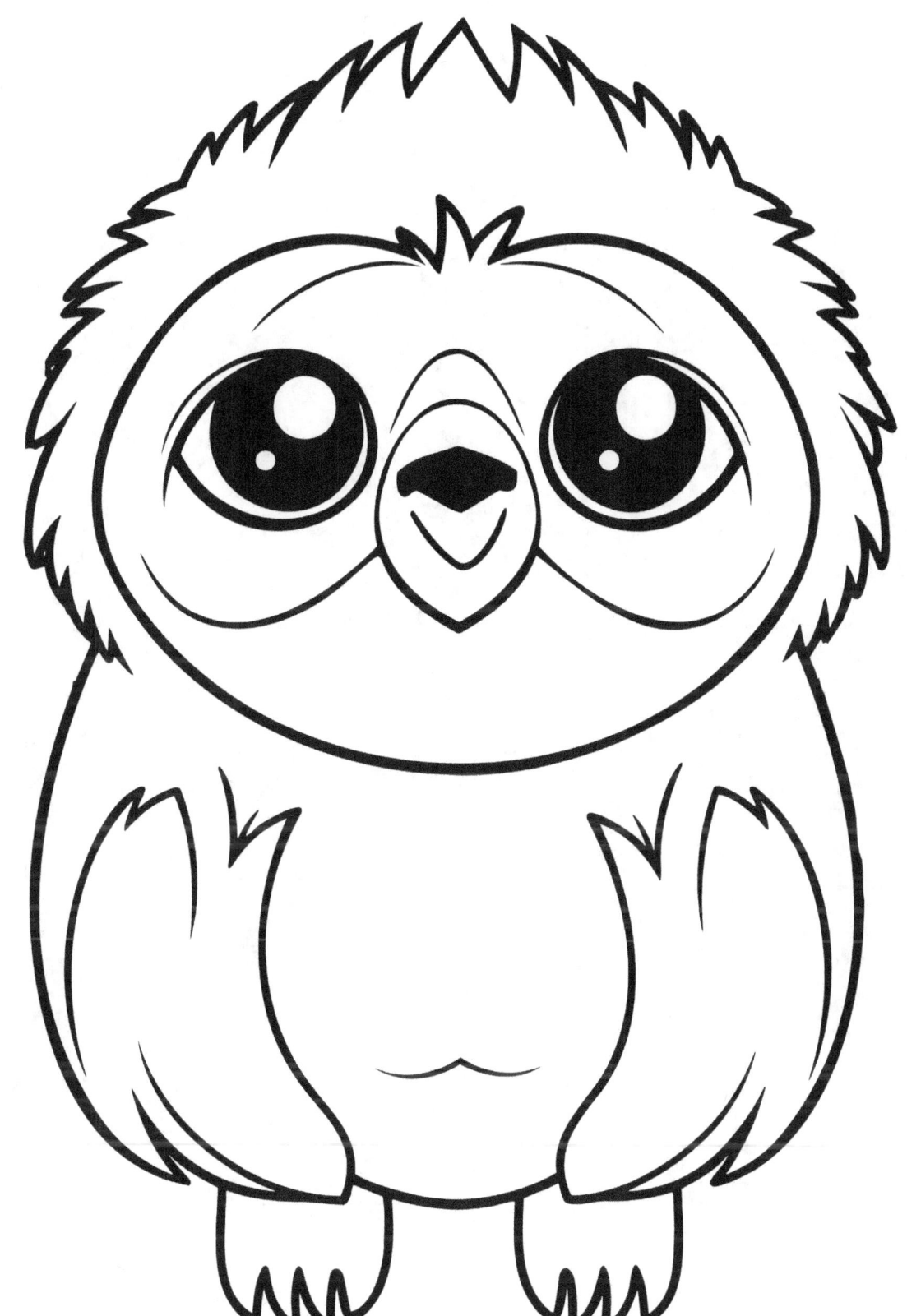

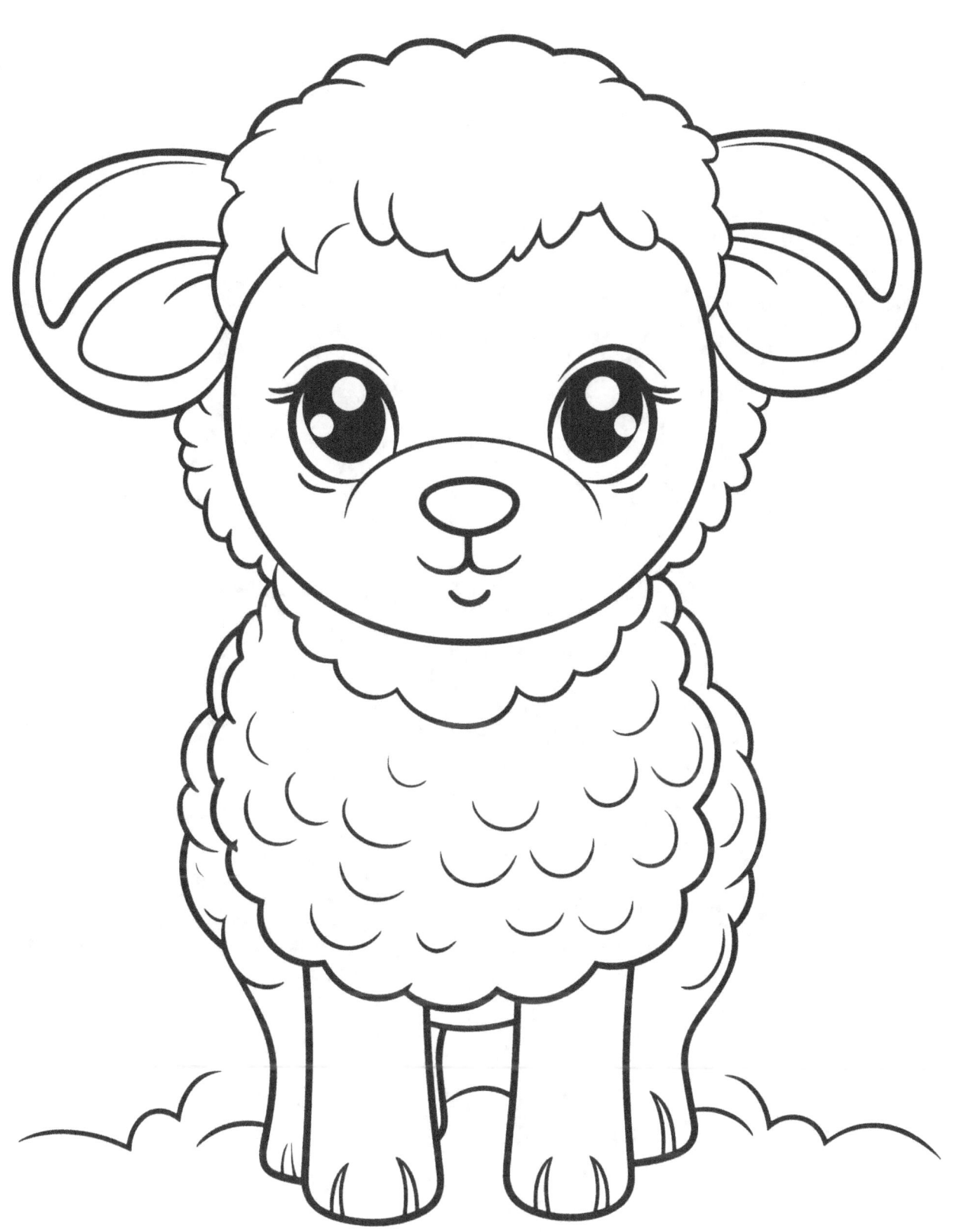

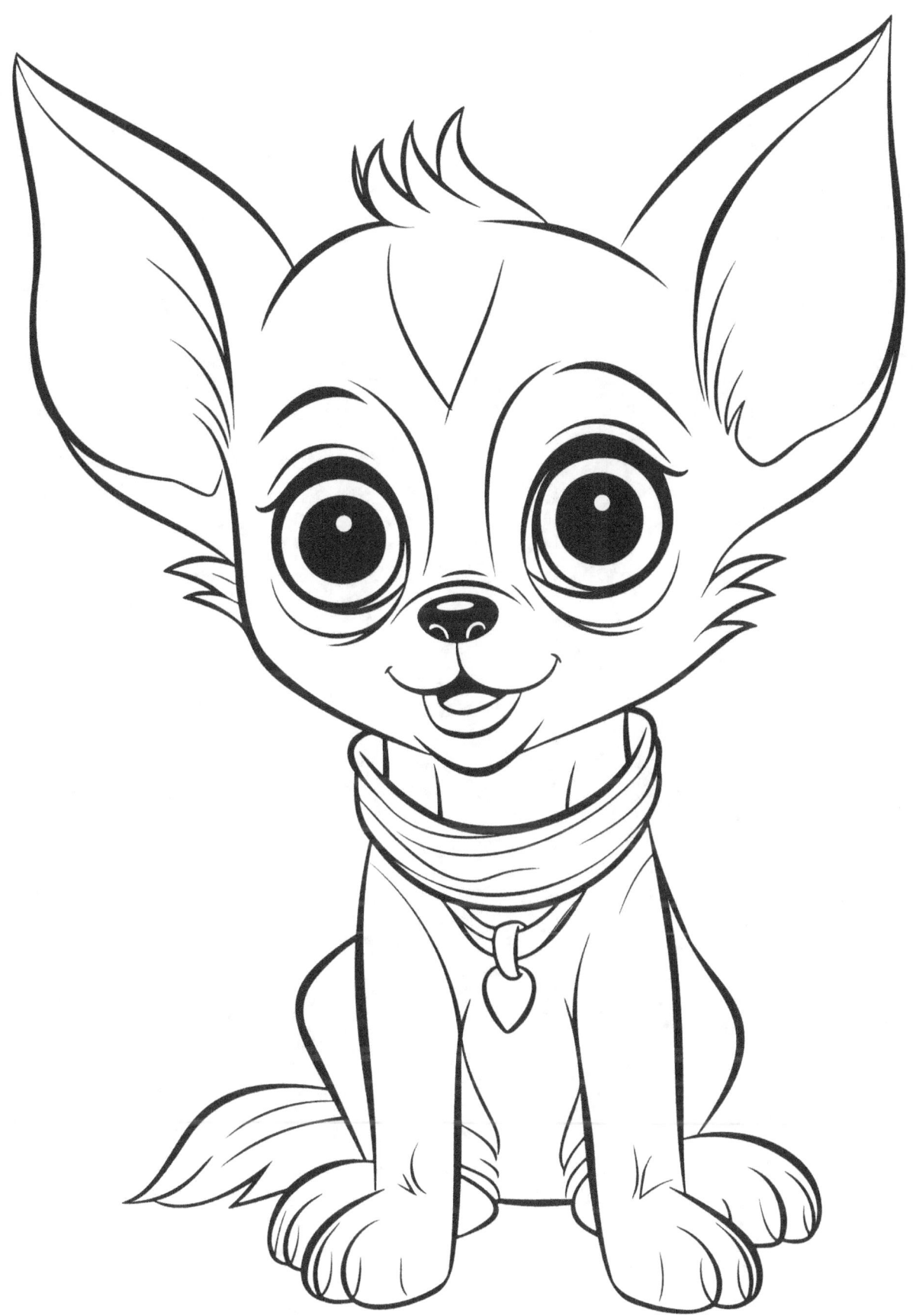

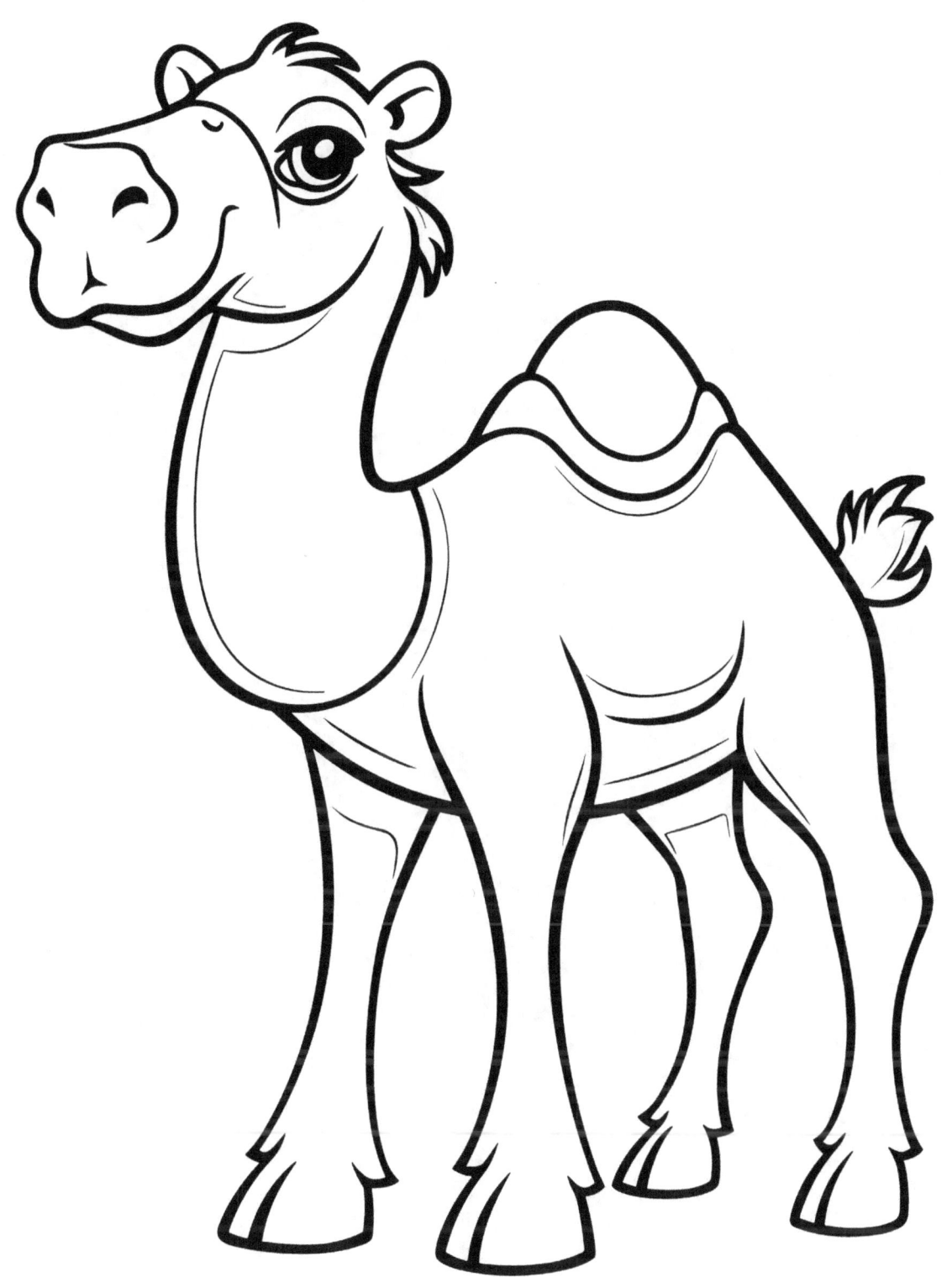

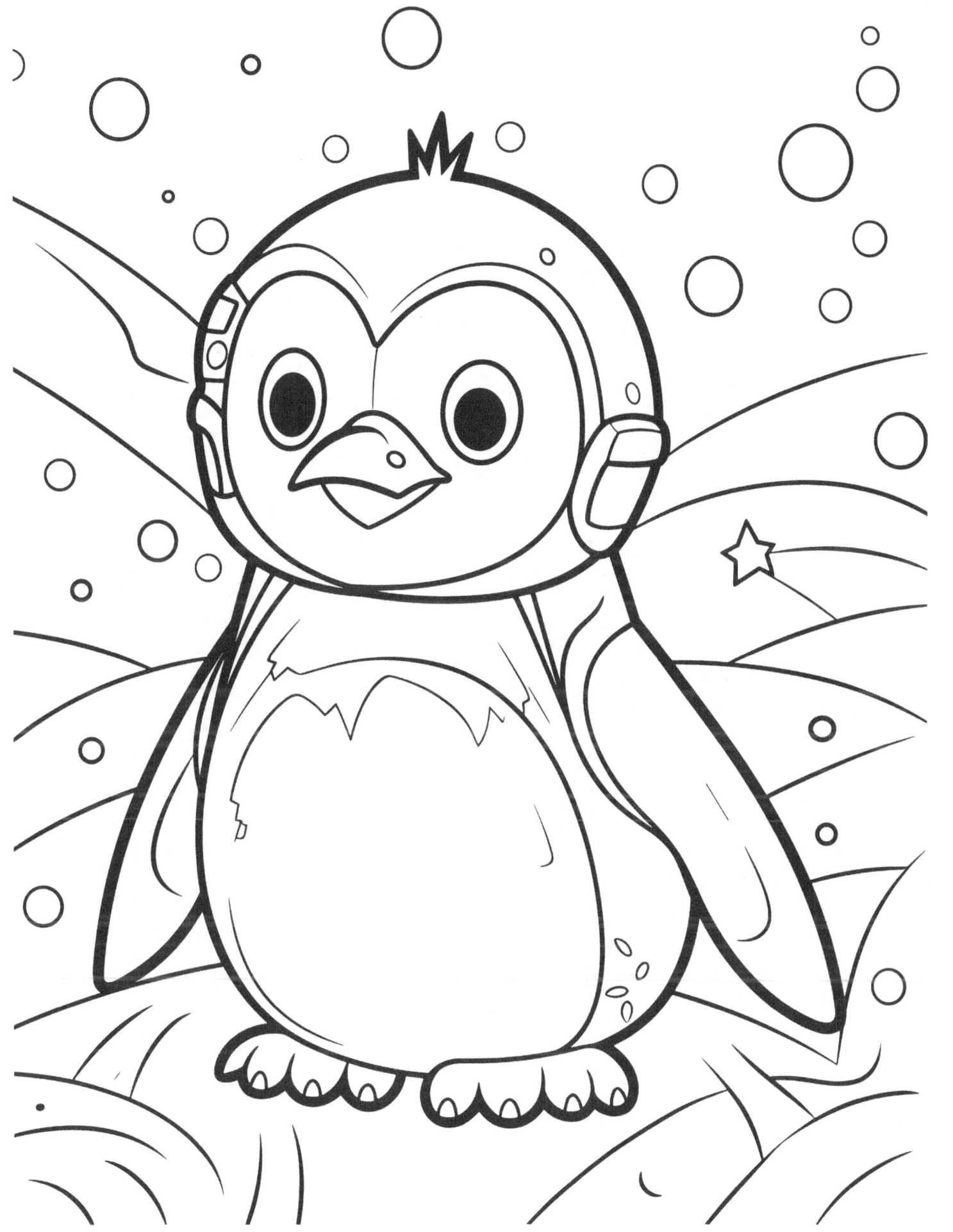

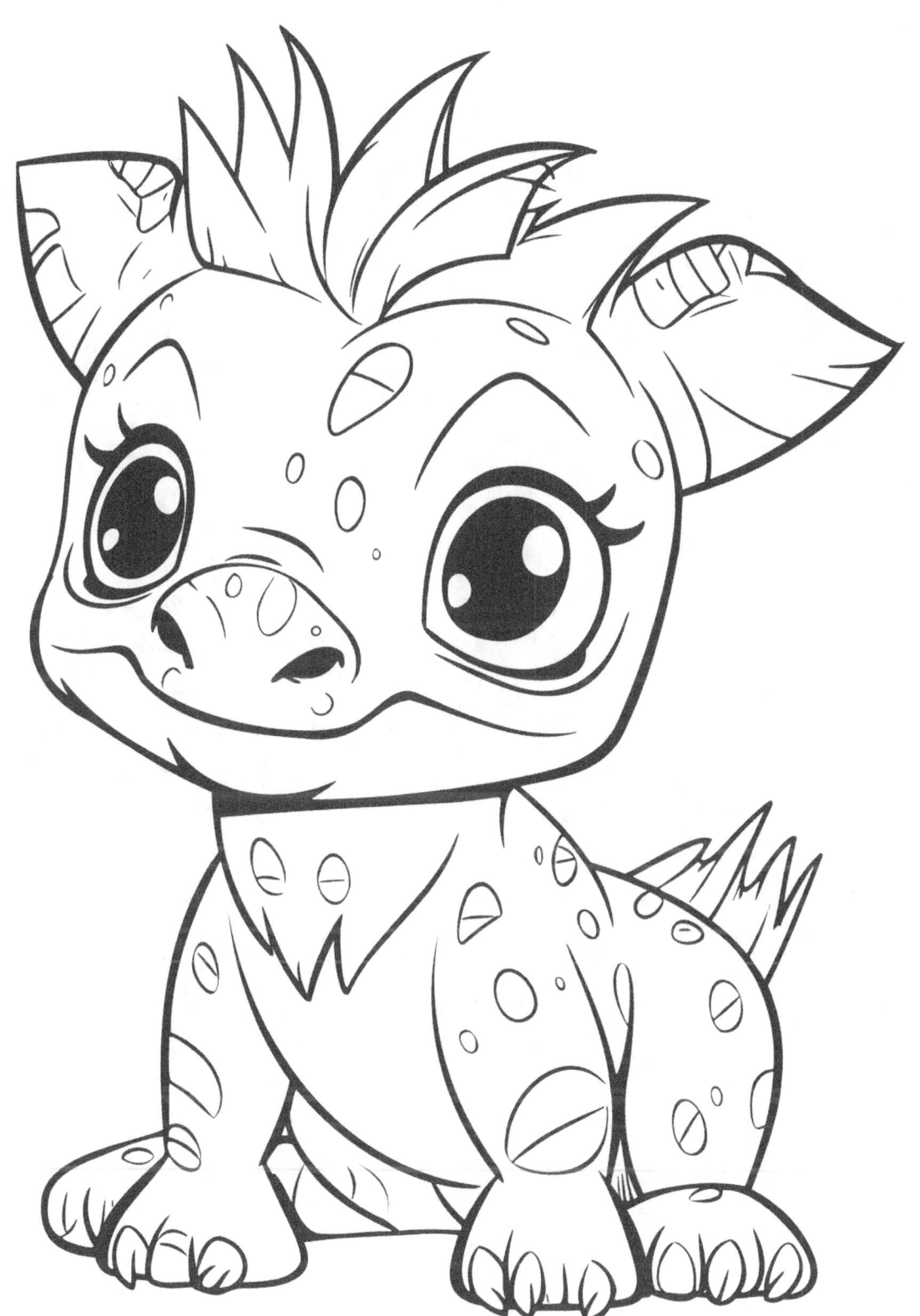

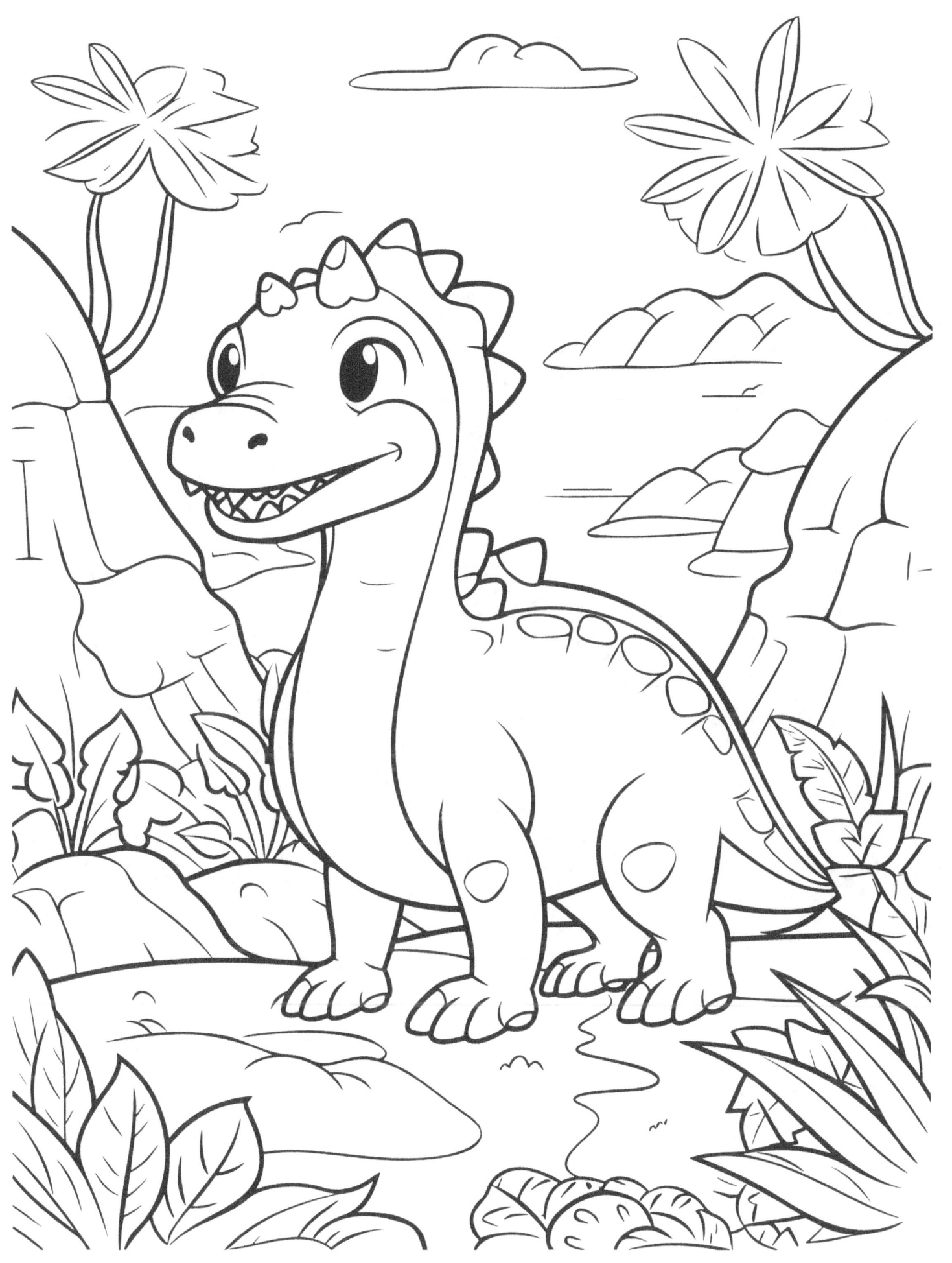

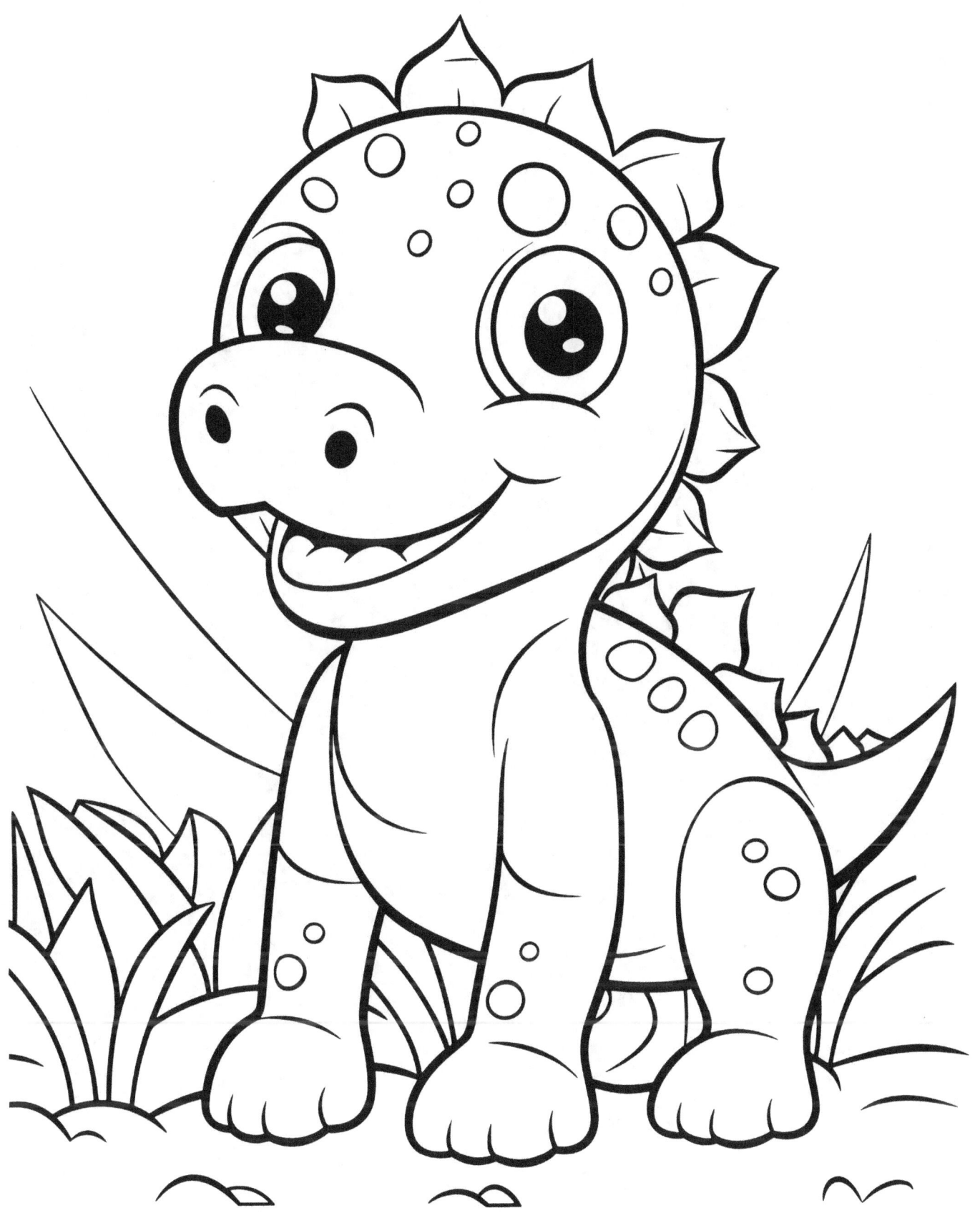

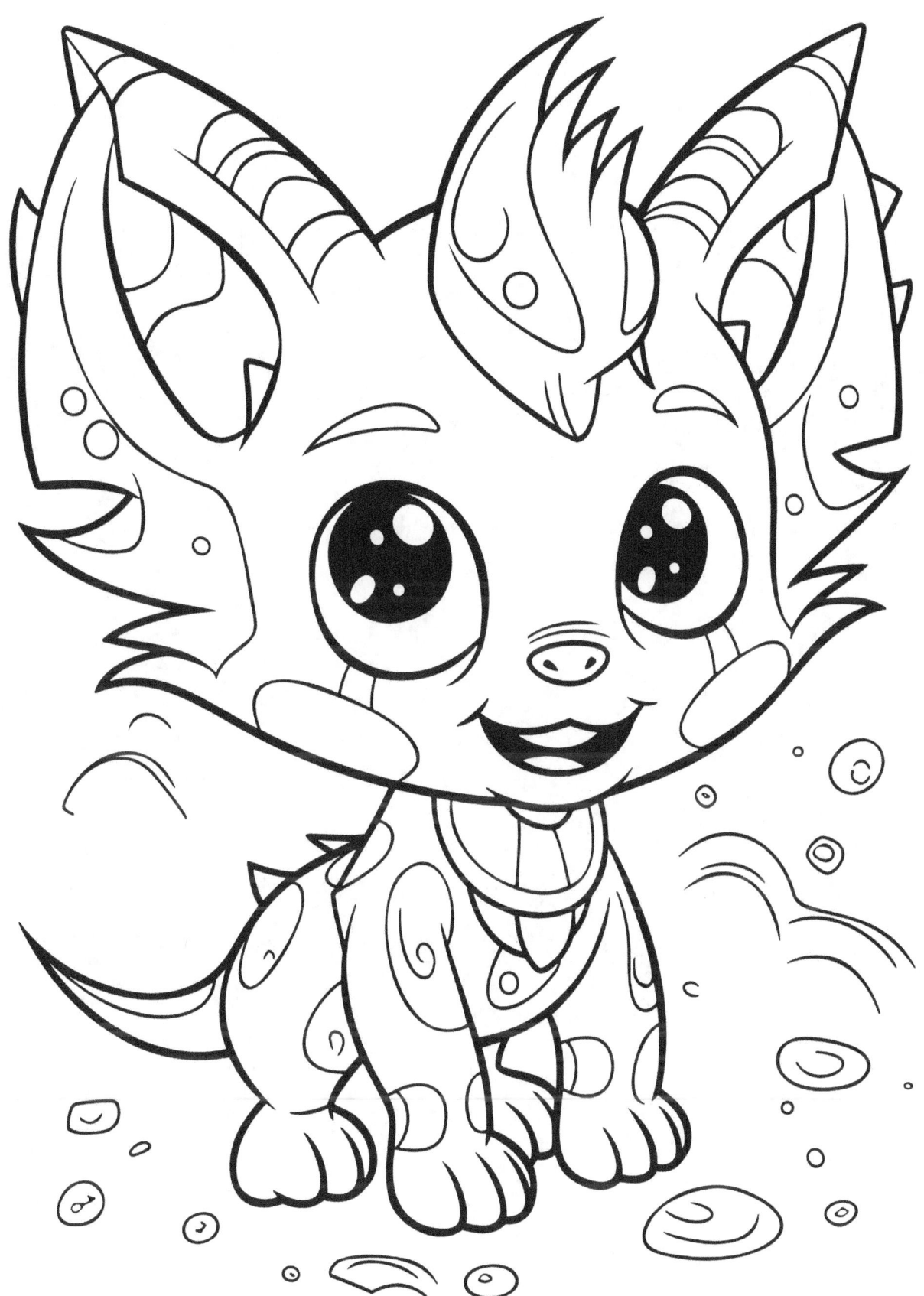

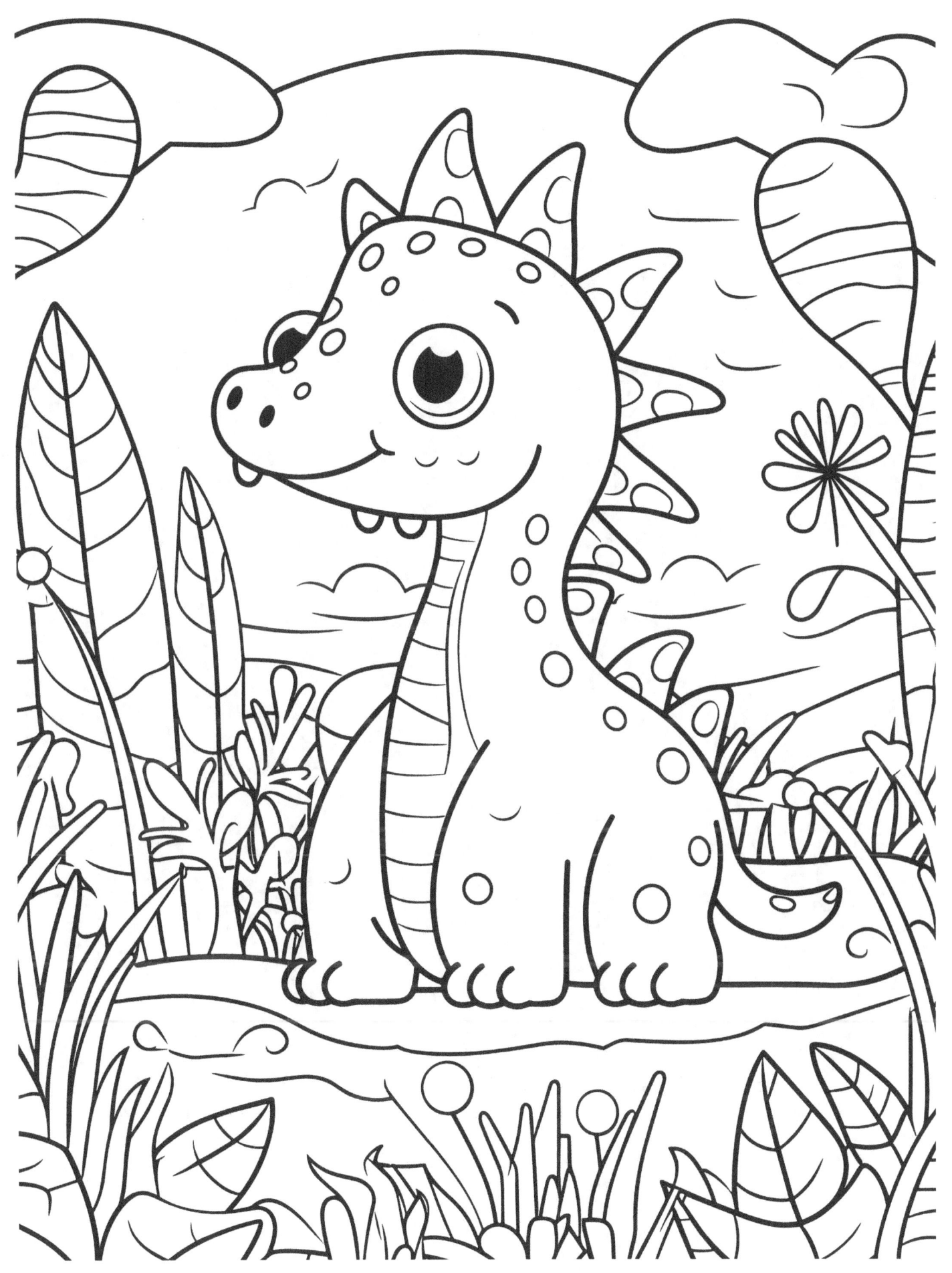

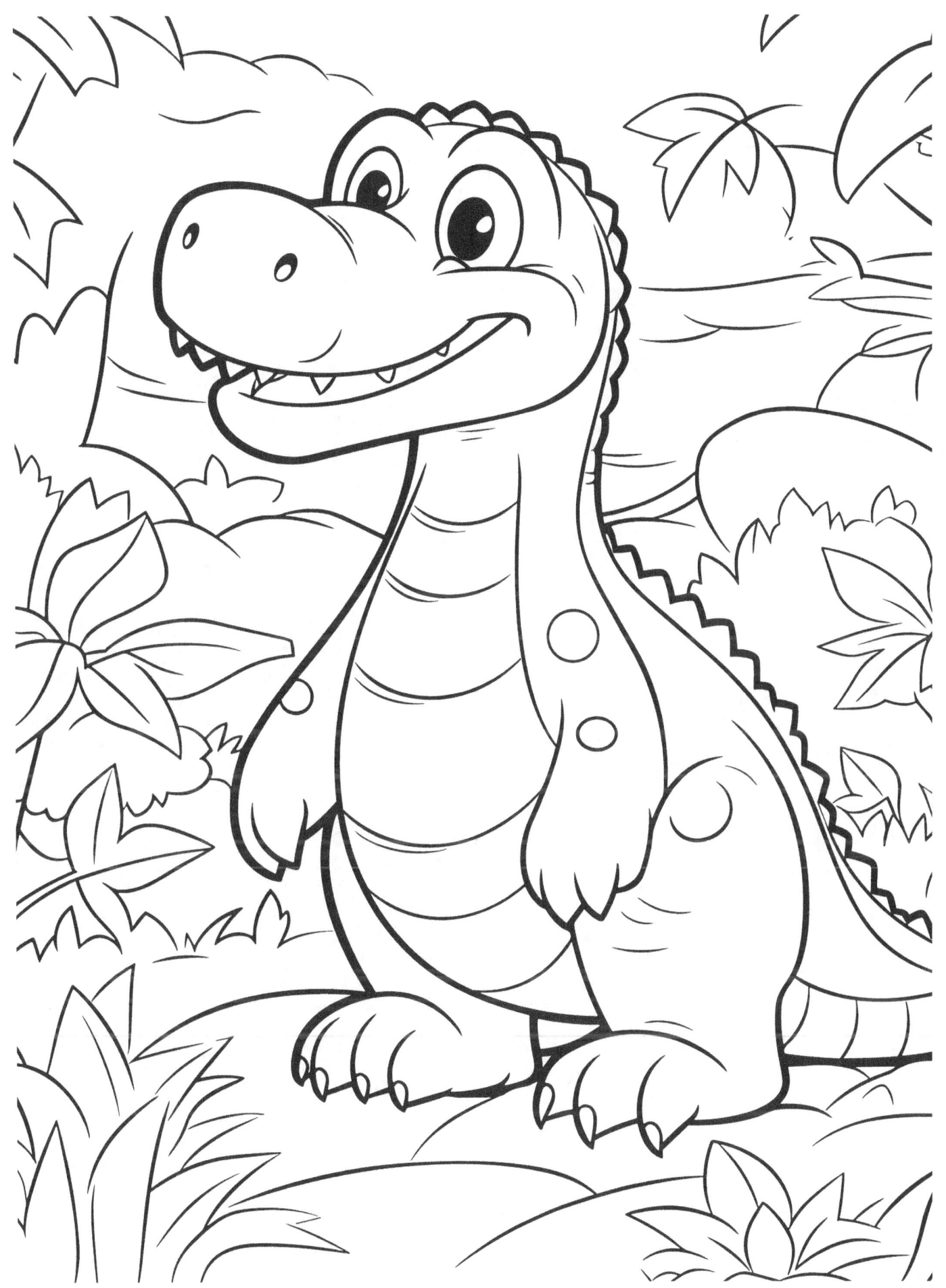

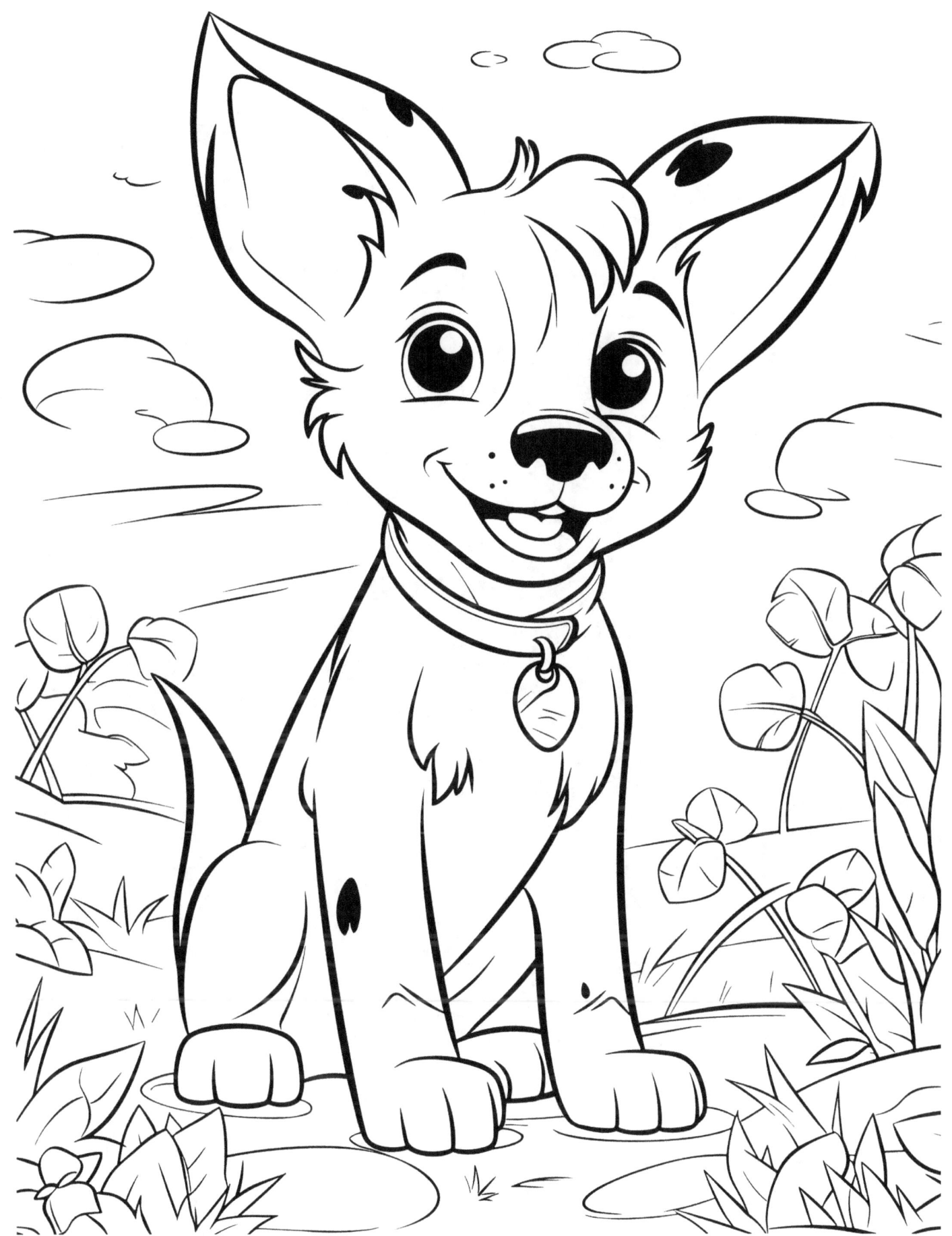

**CONGRATULATIONS, YOU'VE
REACHED THE END!**

It was an amazing adventure!

Take a little break and get ready for the next journey.

There are more delightful coloring books waiting for you from the author